Leadership in
The Digital Age

Leadership in
The Digital Age

Renaissance of
The Renaissance Man

Niklas Hageback

｜￫BEP

BUSINESS EXPERT PRESS

Leader in applied, concise business books

Leadership in The Digital Age: Renaissance of The Renaissance Man
Copyright © Business Expert Press, LLC, 2021.

First published in 2021 by
Business Expert Press, LLC
222 East 46th Street, New York, NY 10017
www.businessexpertpress.com

ISBN-13: 978-1-95253-862-9 (paperback)
ISBN-13: 978-1-95253-863-6 (e-book)

Business Expert Press Collaborative Intelligence Collection

Collection ISSN: 2691-1779 (print)
Collection ISSN: 2691-1795 (electronic)

Cover image licensed by Ingram Image, StockPhotoSecrets.com
Cover and interior design by S4Carlisle Publishing Services Private Ltd., Chennai, India

First edition: 2021

10 9 8 7 6 5 4 3 2 1

Printed in the United States of America.

Dedication

To Aarik and Bernard

Abstract

This is a book for anyone intrigued by the complexities of digital leadership that require a capability to constantly balance the routines of everyday business with the ability to innovate. Finding the appropriate mix between the dichotomy stability and flexibility has been a delicate task that few, if any, corporations have properly managed to overcome. Why is that? This conundrum becomes acute as businesses embark on digital transformations, an often painful venture highlighting the deficiencies of traditional management styles but also agile methodologies. They deliver results that are far below initial expectations, provide half-baked digital solutions where potential commercial gains are poorly captured and leveraged, and, far too often, are not even identified. Mismatches between technologies, the man–machine (dis)connect, or organizational dysfunctionality are typically identified as root causes, but beneath them lurks a more scathing problem: an inadequate leadership.

And it is generally not because of a lack of technological expertise or poor people management that these skills are often sufficiently resourced. The leadership problem is, instead, of a more imperative nature, this as the digital transformation comes to challenge the business to its core: How do we provide customer value, and how do we organize ourselves in the most (cost-)efficient way?

In essence, it takes aim at a corporation's raison d'être and, as such, goes far beyond technical solutions, corporate structure, or indeed even an in-depth understanding of products and markets, this as the digital transformation explicitly (and implicitly) transcends all of these perspectives in its aspiration toward value maximization. By acknowledging these cojoined complexities, elements of what it is that the digital leadership requires can be formulated, namely, a holistic approach capable of incorporating them, facilitated by a cognitive capacity that can craft commercially viable products and services.

But in the age of the specialists that are drilling down in ever more granular minutiae, do there even exist generalists equipped with this holistic mindset, and, if so, what do they look like?

To start with, there are role models that provide inspiration and are worth looking at, but these bring us back a few hundred years in time. **Enter the Renaissance Man.**

Keywords

agile; change management; collective intelligence; creativity; digital leadership; digital transformations; innovation; project management; renaissance man

Contents

Acknowledgments

I would like to express my warmest gratitude to Scott Isenberg and his teams at Business Expert Press and S4Carlisle, respectively, for helping to turn a raw manuscript into a book. I would also like to thank Jim Spohrer, Cognitive OpenTech IBM, for his many valuable comments and insights, which were of great help in my work.

Introduction

Technology alone is not enough. It's technology married with the liberal arts, married with the humanities, that yields us the results that make our hearts sing.

—Steve Jobs, iconic digital leader (1955 to 2011)

The world is in the midst of a digital transformation that is transcending all industries. It is highlighted by two emerging trends that businesses are forced to adhere to:

- All firms are now *technology* firms, whether they acknowledge it or not. This is because upgrades and advances in business models rest on digital solutions, mainly software applications, either developed in-house or third-party tools, customized for bespoke value-added products and services.
- There is a reduced reliance on *quantity* of employees in favor of finding, grooming, and retaining *quality* employees. These typically come with a high level of technological competence, in addition to specific domain expertise. Deploying large numbers of employees to deal with a business challenge is no longer a viable solution, but rather seeking out the extraordinary *man–machine* connect. This is an effect of machines now starting to outmatch large segments of the work force. To fully benefit from these developments, a drastically altered organizational arrangement with a different type of leadership is required.

As a consequence of this changing landscape, most firms are now finding themselves in the proverbial Darwinian survival mode. It is a situation triggered by many factors incidentally acting in concert: fickle customer demands, increased automation at all levels of the organization to push down costs, and growing complexity from operating in fragmented markets defined by differing regulations and heightened political risks. It looks quite like a race to the bottom, with the winner only temporarily taking it all, or at least most of it. But with the low barriers to technical innovation, this dominance is often of a fluid character, and so this race is set to recur over and over again. The assumed longevity of premium branding and customer loyalty is quickly becoming obsolete. In this highly dynamic setting, where change in its many aspects overwhelms all commercial activities, and that too at an accelerating rate, what tools do we have at our disposal to handle and tame it to our advantage? Well, *agile* is currently the buzzword that businesses across industries and geographies hang on to. That agile saw its genesis in the software industry was not by chance. The long development cycles, as prescribed by traditional project management methods, led to deliverables that were often already technically antiquated and way off the mark in terms of functionality at the time of sign-off and deployment. Something more flexible was needed in order to be able to incorporate the ongoing demands for change from customers and increased technical complexity and innovation, features reflecting an industry that was in a constant state of flux. To solve this conundrum, the agile philosophy took aim at two key principles:

- Keep bureaucracy at a minimum by, as far as possible, eliminating formal process and protocol, and
- Break down hierarchies and flatten the organization with a focus on concentrated cross-functional teamwork, which can include the end users, empowered with executive decision-making power.

Although straightforward, agile practices keep everyone on their toes. Daily sprints ensure that no slackers need apply and that everyone is held accountable for their productivity. Thus, they are highly demanding yet well endowed if properly performed. Numerous testimonies agree on how products have come to much more closely reflect the customers' actual needs and are delivered in a notably faster and more labor-efficient manner. Agile, in its many variations, is therefore now an acclaimed project management standard. But like previous popular project- and strategic management concepts that eventually faded into oblivion, is the same fate also awaiting the agile framework?

The author argues that it appears to be different this time. The popularity of agile has given it a longevity that has by far extended that of some of its predecessors, such as Six Sigma, Just in Time, and Balanced Scorecards. Agile, or rather the agile mindset, is here to stay simply because the conditions that brought it forth in the first place, including fast-paced change, have now become the milieu for almost all industries. It is something they will have to adjust to for the foreseeable future, and agile is by far the best tool we have at our disposal to handle it. But agile has limitations, and there are still missing components. The cross-functional teams, with their wide variety of perspectives, are requiring a new type of leadership, namely, a generalist leader, an individual well versed in all relevant knowledge domains, not only technology. It is someone able to comprehend a digital transformation in all its facets and to ensure that potential commercial exploits can be fully capitalized on. Indeed, a very different managerial proposition than the currently preferred specialist manager, who is still being touted in business education. In essence, it is a leadership style with roots reaching back to medieval times, and we are seeing the return of the illustrious *Renaissance Man*.

Agile, given its flexible attributes, is extending beyond project management to include business development, and, more recently, an agile organizational template is seeking to find its form. But will it work? The publicized success stories of triumphant and superior agile organizations have appeared suspiciously few and far between. It certainly does not tally with agile consultants' tall claims of its perceived advantages. Somehow, it appears difficult to fully endorse agile, and a certain amount of bureaucracy and procrastination in decision-making and execution appears inevitable for big corporations. It is possibly the result of an inherent condition in all forms of human collectives that we keep falling back on despite efforts to circumvent these traits. Aspiring to do considerably more with less is an amicable proposition, but by its very nature, it implicitly seeks to eliminate a lot of corporate bureaucracy that is occupied by the middle management cadre. This poses a grave threat to the career man who is considered the backbone of many corporations. It has become a battle between governing philosophies that is now being fought in many corporate boardrooms, and the short-term outcome is far from certain. One thing appears clear, however: Agile is here to stay, but in what forms and at what organizational layers are questions that remain unanswered. So if agile is unable to go all the way, are there alternatives and should they be considered? Perhaps the concept of collective intelligence can augment initiatives to embrace both innovation and the digital transformation of a corporation.

The vast scale and enormous magnitude of this digital transformation paradigm shift that is now unraveling is not only changing work and management structures in the commercial world but will also affect society as a whole. Can the acclaimed benefits that have been reaped at the corporate and industry levels also materialize at the societal level? Are we standing on the threshold of a beautiful new world enabled by digital technologies, or are there unforeseen consequences that mean that we have inadvertently been nurturing a Frankenstein's monster about to be unleashed?

This book consists of five chapters:

Chapter 1: The Accelerating Pace of Change

The economic circumstances have, over the last century, progressed dramatically—from Henry Ford's assembly line principles with standardized products offered to potential customers, who simply had to accept what was on display, to the current highly individualized expressions of consumerism. This trend is now advancing further through the digital economy. Global brands have come to realize that purchasing preferences are capricious and that relying on consumer loyalty, based on a previous glorious past, is at their own peril. The pace of technological innovations interchangeably interacts with market demands, feeding off each other in symbiosis. Any corporation unwilling to adopt and embrace this reality will soon find itself sharing the destiny of the dinosaurs, a fate that no slick marketing campaign can rescue it from. However, the forces of change from customers as well as a combination of economic, political, regulatory, technical and even cultural trends has created a mosaic of complexities that are now eclipsing all industries. It obligates them, both explicitly and implicitly, to an *Agilian* approach that only perhaps will enable them to remain competitive. It is beginning to dawn on most executives that the sense of being in control is nowadays merely a hazy illusion.

Chapter 2: Agile and then Some More Agile

That the agile framework was first adopted in the software industry was evolutionary, because frequent change requests had become a way of life for them. Eventually, they had to respond to the volatile environment. Hence, the advent of the Agile Manifesto. Although change was also accelerating in other industries, it was fitting that it took off in software development, because it was a relatively new industry where cultural institutions and folklore had not yet firmly formed and risked stagnating business practices. The positive impacts of applying agile methodologies on project works have been well documented, but are its principles also applicable at the organizational level? With markets in constant change in terms of new goods and services being introduced, and others becoming outdated at an unprecedented pace, the answer is assumed to be an affirmative. However, its success at the micro level has by and large failed to materialize at the macro level. Transforming a whole corporation to live and breathe by the agile ethos has proven difficult, and in most cases too difficult. Although there is no dearth of corporates claiming to be agile throughout, a closer look reveals that many employees, and indeed whole functions, are often only paying lip service. They still do things just the way they have always been doing them. Why has agile proven so hard to implement outside the IT function? Is it a lack of tangible deliverables and measurable metrics that makes it difficult to practically implement? Or is there a clash between the personality types thriving in bureaucracies and the philosophy that underpins agile? A hard-earned insight into many practitioners is that regardless of exquisitely drafted strategies, the success of agile rests on its employees' capabilities and willingness to truly embrace and live by its principles. This is something that has proven easier said than done, because it is commonly acknowledged to be an intense and demanding form of working, and clearly not suitable for everyone. Most business executives and psychologists do agree that it is more about mindset than about understanding the framework, which itself is fairly uncompli- cated. This brings agile's most contentious issue to the forefront: Can this mindset be taught or is there an innate agile personality?

Chapter 3: The Innovating Organization

There is a growing acceptance that agile will work for some part of the organization, but really not at all for others. A broad-brush delineation can be made between bureaucratic functions focused on control and en- suring compliance with various regulations on one side. These are defined by stability and conformity, and a general risk-averse attitude is the pre- ferred personal skill set sought after, something to which agile can do little and can actually be detrimental. On the other side, business units are operating in turbulent environments where embracing calculated risks and developing commercial ventures through innovation are decisive for success. Here, agile has proven to be an important tool to accommodate these creative aspirations and leverage the opportunities that might arise. The ability to innovate has come to be one of the key defining success factors in the digital economy, but can it be facilitated? What organiza- tional form is most suited to optimizing the arrangement of employees' creative abilities and competencies? The innovating organization strikes at the very core of the digital age, and corporations able to incorporate its features in their day-to-day operations will lead rather than follow, an enormous advantage in unpredictable consumer markets.

Chapter 4: The Renaissance Man

As businesses embark on digital transformations, it often becomes appar- ent that the traditional management styles are not performing satisfac- torily, delivering results that are far below initial expectations, providing half-baked digital solutions where potential commercial gains are poorly captured and leveraged and far too often not even identified. Mismatches between technologies, the man–machine (dis-)connect, or organizational dysfunctionality are typically identified as root causes, but beneath them lurks a more scathing problem: an inadequate leadership. This inadequacy rests on a lack of holistic insights backed by well-rounded skills and sets of knowledge that are required to understand all aspects of a digital transformation, including the stakeholders concerned—employees and customers. What is required to meet these challenges is a modern take of the *Renaissance Man*.

Chapter 5: A Beautiful New World?

The ongoing digital transformations are all-encompassing in that they are disrupting all industries in all geographies, and governmental agencies and bureaucracies are no exceptions. But what is the cumulative impact on society at large? Are we experiencing a bottom-up revolution? Is it a leap into the unknown with unfolding and little known consequences for education, the labor market, and the welfare system; and what about demographics? And can it also extend to politics? Are we set for an unavoidable conflict between top-down authoritarian governing models and the digital transformations that, by design, seek to break down hierarchies?

CHAPTER 1

The Accelerating Pace of Change

Change before you have to.

—Jack Welch,
American business leader (1935 to 2020)

With Industrialization Came Standardization

For the industrialization phase, commencing in the later part of the 19th century, to at all take off, mass production enabled by standardization was a necessity. It was accompanied by polished marketing campaigns (for the time) that titillated the demand for products that consumers often did not know existed or that they actually had any genuine need for. It was an enormous success, fueling economic growth that provided purchasing power to both a spiraling working class and an emerging middle class, rising from hordes of farm hands and kitchen maids. It was the first time in history really that the *plebeians* of society could so drastically improve their lives, materially at least. The man behind the managerial principles that came to form so much of the industrial era was the American engineer Frederick Winslow Taylor (1856 to 1915), the key tenets outlined in his book *The Principles of Scientific Management* from 1911. The book succinctly summed up the breakthrough insights that would optimize labor productivity using Taylor's scientific method and came to dominate industrial thinking for much of the century. His method allowed for unprecedented effectiveness and efficiency, as it took aim at mass production and quality control organized through hierarchy and specialization. It was the American industrialist Henry Ford (1863 to 1947) who perfected mass production by applying the assembly-line principle on car manufacturing. Corporations were aptly depicted as mechanical systems, with employees being small cogs in a big wheel. Workers, as much as the consumers, were easily replaceable; hence, the era of industrialism saw numerous clashes between labor unions and employers to establish what minimum worker's rights should include. The assembly-line principles were adapted by most industries, albeit in various degrees, with standardization becoming the zeitgeist extending also into art and architecture. The streamlined Art Deco and Bauhaus replaced the pre-World War I free-wielding school of Art Nouveau. In all, there was little room allowed for individuality; basically it was a "one-size-fits-all" culture, famously highlighted in Ford's car selling slogan "*chose any color you like as long as it is black.*" The murkier aspects of this standardization mania were found in politics and notably both socialism and fascism sought to eliminate all traits of individualism and create the political mass man. In a bizarre manner, it somehow complemented capitalism's commercial mass man. In the end, it came with disastrous consequences for anyone falling outside the norms of political standardization. It found its ultimate sinister expressions in the concentration camps of World War II, as well as Soviet and Chinese communism's *gulags*, genocides which have left deep scars on the human soul that have remained till date. This was truly assembly-line murder factories working in overdrive, attempting to eradicate all tendencies that deviated from the ideal man template, not only physically but also in terms of political inclinations, and implicitly their consumer tastes and preferences. After World War II, with the horrors of collectivism being fully exposed, the consumers in the free world started to prioritize individual choices and preferences ahead of standardized products. Trend-sensitive corporations quickly adjusted themselves by starting to offer a wide variety of goods and services that defined the consumerism frenzy of the 1950s and 1960s. Although the managerial and organizational principles of Taylorism largely remained, over time it would prove incompatible to match the demand of such erratic consumers. The early 1950s saw a new industrial revolution commencing with the birth of a product that would herald the change to come—computers.[1,2]

The Advent of Agile

The software development life cycle at the early days of the computer industry typically followed rigid project steps that it rarely deviated from. These include the following:

- the collation and gathering of requirements;
- the functional design phase of the software;
- the testing and verification of functionality;
- deployment; and finally
- the maintenance of the software.

Every step of the project life cycle had to be completed and approved before the ensuing phase could commence. If it was discovered that some changes were needed, the entire project had to revert to the initial step, and the cycle had to be redone and reapproved. It goes without saying that this project methodology was exceptionally cumbersome, inflexible, and end heavy in terms of deliverables. Users would typically have to wait for years to see the final product. It came to be labeled the waterfall methodology, reflecting the strict step-by-step approach. It had its origin in engineering and was adequate for its time, as technological innovations and upgrades that triggered change requests were relatively rare. But, from the late 1970s onward, software applications were starting to become more complicated. The first personal computers had become available and introduced to households and workplaces. Developers started to realize the limitations of the waterfall project methodology, and its iterative steps slowed down the software development considerably. More and more change requests were appearing throughout the project cycle, which were driven by the rapid advancement of technological innovations and demand for new functionality from the end-users. By the early 1990s, software development teams started to feel overwhelmed, having trouble keeping up with all the changes coming through. It came to be known as the application delivery lag. Experts in the industry estimated that the average time between a validated business need and the requested application being tested and launched for deployment was about three years. Within that time frame, functionality, systems, and even entire industries were likely to have undergone changes, sometimes dramatically so. A lot of software were in fact already antiquated by the time of being introduced to their intended users. The verdict was out; the waterfall project methodology could not adequately adapt to the increased pace and the complexity of the change requests. It simply was not designed to deliver applications fast enough or respond effectively to the required changes that arose throughout the projects. But the waterfall methodology was deeply rooted in many practitioners' mentality, living by the devise; that the more time you spent planning, the less time you spend writing code, and the better that code would be. It was a hallmark of the reigning engineering ethos, deliberately process- and documentation heavy, where the emphasis was put on meticulous planning, which made a lot of sense for the construction business. But the challenges that software engineers and programmers now were facing had started to deviate considerably from the requirements of building roads and houses. Software projects no longer had its previous stability in terms of requirements and they had to be concluded a lot quicker than the previous years-long durations. To this came the insight that the requirements of what the software applications were supposed to be doing were never that exact versus the requirements of constructing a bridge or similar. There was always a bit of guesswork involved, and that by default meant that as the project proceeded some change requirements were inevitable. Typically, end-users could approximate the workflows, but it was never a precise model of the real world. The programmers were at times forced to second guess what to automate and how the applications really should work, and of course there were bound to be discrepancies.[3,4] Hence, the programmer community began exploring new ways to approach software development. In the 1990s, a group of thought leaders developed a project management methodology that was more adapted to quickly react and respond to both change requests and technological upgrades. Various variations dawned, and in the early 2000s, the concept of agile software development was borne to describe the flexible nature of the development cycle. The pressures coming from a steady stream of technological innovations and the increased pace of change requests were now seen not only in the software business but also in many other industries, such as automotive and aerospace manufacturing. They started to consider this alternative approach, as, for instance, the design time of a new car was cut almost in half in the 1990s, compared to the previous duration of six years; a quicker way of getting things done was necessary. In 2001, at a meeting in the resort town of Snowbird, Utah, some leading software practitioners published the *Manifesto for Agile Software Development.*[5] The gist of the agile methodology is to enable project teams to quickly build working software and get it into the hands of end-users. Rapid feedback and a willingness to change have turned out to be key success factors. Little is set in stone at the beginning of the project, so if the project team is not entirely sure of the user needs, they first deliver an approximation and then collect feedback, making adjustments accordingly. The pioneers of agile gave some guiding tenets:

- Individuals and interactions precede processes and tools;
- Focus on building software over comprehensive documentation;
- Prioritize customer collaboration over contract negotiation, and;
- Quickly respond to change over following a plan.[6]

Most agile methods break the product development work into small increments that minimize the preplanning phase of the project. The work of the agile teams is assessed in regular meetings called daily sprints. These are accumulated into relatively short time frames, or timeboxes, that typically last from one to four weeks. They involve a cross-functional team covering all key functions: planning, analysis, design, coding, unit testing, and acceptance testing. At the end of each of these sprint periods, a minimum viable product (MVP) is presented to the stakeholders. This approach effectively reduces the overall project risk and allows the product development team to respond quickly to any required changes. A sprint might not add enough functionality to merit a formal release, but the objective is to have the aforementioned MVP available with hopefully few, if any, bugs. Typically, multiple sprints are required to release a software application, or new features. To ensure that the emphasis is on getting things done, the delivery of functioning software is the primary performance metric. It has proved to work particularly well for complex software as well as product development projects that hold dynamic and nondeterministic characteristics.[7,8]

So, what are then the main differences between the agile project methodology and the waterfall project methodology? Basically, the agile approach breaks down the project by creating several smaller deliverables that come to form the envisaged product, and which are likely to differ, sometimes considerably so, than what was initially expected. In the waterfall model, the deliverables are exactly planned at the onset of the project with the expectation of few deviations. The testing of the software is a separate step that follows the development step, whereas in agile, the coding and testing are completed in the same sprint. Therefore, the project setup has to adjust to the product rather than vice versa.[9] Summarizing all these insights, The Agile Manifesto included 12 principles:

1. Deliver customer satisfaction by delivering valuable software continuously.
2. Always accept change of requirements no matter how early or late in the project.
3. Deliver software that works within a shorter timescale.
4. Both developers and business professionals must work closely together daily throughout the duration of the project.
5. Information is best transferred between parties in face-to-face conversations.
6. Motivate people to build a project by creating an environment of appreciation, trust, and empowerment.
7. Working software is the key measure of progress.
8. The agile process promotes sustainable development.
9. Continuous attention to excellence and quality in technical development and design boosts the agility.
10. Simplicity is a vital part of effective agile management.
11. Self-organized teams produce the best architecture, requirements, and design.
12. Teams should reflect through inspection and adaptation to be more effective.[10]

However, since the launch of agile, certain criticisms have emerged:

- Despite its intentions, it has often proven to be more developer-centric rather than user-centric.
- The transition from waterfall methods to agile is challenging, as employees can fail to adapt to the new mindset required.
- It focuses more on the (functional) requirements and code development rather than on product design, which sometimes needs a holistic approach. It happens typically when developing large-scale complex products, such as airplanes and spacecraft.
- Agile methodologies are sometimes incompatible in large organizations, as they are being prevented from true deployment due to heavy bureaucracy and vested interests that seek to uphold the status quo not approving of the method's flexible arrangements.[11]

Agile methodologies will generally fail to work, not due to faulty implementation of the framework itself, which by any standard is rather simplistic, but through a lack of stakeholder commitment. The corporations' collective mindset, including key decision-makers, both formal and informal, may only pay lip service when endorsing the agile philosophy. This as they come to the realization that they are not capable or willing to live by it. A lack of support from executives means that agile methodologies are often implemented bottom-up by true enthusiasts and then confined only to development teams, possibly extending elsewhere in the IT department but rarely beyond that. Herein lies an accountability problem in large organizations, as if only small teams or functions adhere to it, its work practices will often come in conflict with other managerial and organizational models. Given the high intensity and focus that agile sprints demand, team members can then not spend the required time to meet their objectives, by being engaged in various aspects of the corporate bureaucracy. Key insights to a successful agile implementation highlight the need for capable individuals across different disciplines that can quickly act on change requests, and this in a nonhierarchical management style. While tools and processes are important, more important still is to have the right mindset to handle all these changes that can be expected and also proactively generated. Whether there is an agile mindset, perhaps innate, is a critical question that will be discussed in a later chapter.[12] In practice though and particularly in larger corporations, hybrid models combining elements of agile and waterfall are often deployed, making projects more document- and preplanning-heavy than what the pure agile methodology prescribes.[13]

Scrum

Originating from the overarching agile framework are several subsets, out of which one of the most popular is scrum. The term is borrowed from the sport of rugby, where players with different roles come together in team collaboration to restart a halted game seeking to gain control over the ball. The scrum methodology is backed by a quite extensive body of research that has shown that the 'best' results occur when small project teams are allowed to self-organize and operate against objectives to which they have the freedom to decide way forward, this rather than being given specific assignments and micro-managed. Scrum techniques have been calibrated for small teams, typically no more than nine project members. The edifice of scrum rests on three pillars, namely transparency, inspection, and adaptation, which allows it to respond to feedback timely. These three pillars require trust and openness in the team, which the following five values of scrum seek to promote:

1. *Commitment:* Team members individually commit to achieving their team goals, each and every sprint.
2. *Courage:* Team members know they have the courage to work through conflict and challenges together so that they can do the right thing.
3. *Focus:* Team members focus exclusively on their team goals and the sprint backlog; there should be no work done other than through their backlog.
4. *Openness:* Team members and their stakeholders agree to be transparent about their work and any challenges they face.
5. *Respect:* Team members respect each other to be technically capable and to work with good intent.[14]

The project work is broken down into sprints, no longer than one month in duration, and its progress is tracked in daily stand-up meetings, called daily scrums (typically around 15 minutes). During the daily scrum, each team member is expected to be prepared to respond to three questions:

- What did I complete yesterday that contributed to the team meeting our sprint goal?
- What do I plan to complete today to contribute to the team meeting our sprint goal?
- Do I see any impediment that could prevent me or the team from meeting our sprint goal?

Through these ongoing scrums, the project team should be able to identify early on if and when their work starts to deviate and needs to be steered back on path to keep the progression going.[15,16] One of the key scrum tools is the product backlog, which is a model of the work to be done and includes an ordered list of the product requirements. User stories are deployed, which being only a couple of sentences long aim to capture a description of a software feature from the end-user perspective. This is done by highlighting the type of user, what they want and why, seeking to create a simplified description of a requirement.[17] There are three key roles in a scrum project that differ from the traditional project management setup: product owner, scrum master, and team members. The product owner oversees all the business requirements to ensure the right product functionalities are being built and executed correctly. The product owner is required to be able to prioritize and negotiate change requests, maintain good working relations with the project team and stakeholders, and ultimately have both the authority and integrity to make decisions about the project. The role is critical as it represents the business, typically also the customers, and the functionality they seek, something that requires intense interaction with the development team. But in real life, it often happens that the product owners cannot dedicate enough time, as they often are far too busy focusing on their business activities, whether that be sales, business development, or serving clients. Similarly, the team members can be drawn into other engagements, such as having to involve in unplanned RAD (rapid application development) activities or software support and maintenance. This lack of allocating sufficient time is one of the main sources of failure in scrum projects.

The scrum master's role is more of a coach rather than project manager, helping the project team work effectively together in accordance with the scrum principles. It is very much a hands-on role where the scrum master helps the team by removing anything that can impair performance, facilitates meetings, keeps tab on progress, and is in charge of handling general problem-solving but typically does not have people management responsibilities. In short, the scrum master is expected to be an expert on the scrum framework and the various tools deployed. The scrum master ultimately acts as a buffer between the team and any distracting influences. It is a role that can coexist side by side with the project manager who is in charge of project scope, cost, personnel, risk management, and other typical project manager responsibilities.

One of the most important roles beyond the educational aspect, and one of the well-documented key success factors of the scrum methodology, is the promotion of self-organization and cross-functionality within the project team. The team members themselves are expected to be empowered to lead this effort, with the scrum master's role solely being of an advisory nature. It is also one of the most sensitive points, as it challenges, and sometimes confronts, existing career hierarchies. So, finding a workable synergy between product owner, scrum master, and team members is a decisive factor that comes to determine much of a scrum project's success.[18,19]

Some of the limitations of the scrum methodology have been found to be as follows:

- Problems can arise when the team cannot physically sit together and/or are only involved part-time, having to simultaneously manage competing tasks. Scrum advocates close an ongoing interaction, as that enables the perceived "sum is more than the components" effect.
- If team members lack well-rounded skills and are merely highly specialized in single-domain expertise areas, the cross-functional self-organizing effect might not arise as disparate jargons and narratives hinder connectivity.
- Products with many external dependencies. The scrum methodology rests on dividing product developments into short sprints, out of which some might come with plenty of external dependencies,

such as user acceptance testing or coordination with other teams. These can lead to delays and the failure of individual sprints, putting the whole project at risk.

• Products that are mature, or legacy, needing an upgrade, or have required regulated quality controls are less suitable, as in scrum, product increments should be fully developed and tested in a single sprint. Products that need large amounts of safety testing or similar, such as medical devices, components for airplanes, or nuclear power plants, for each release are therefore better suited for the waterfall methodology.[20]

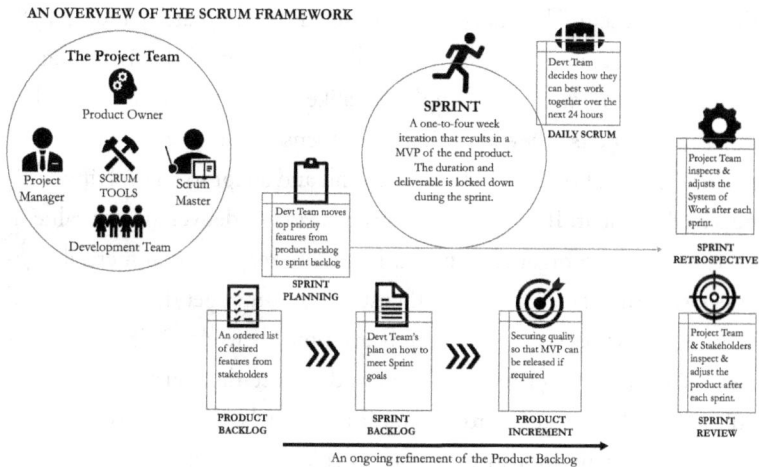

AN OVERVIEW OF THE SCRUM FRAMEWORK

Figure 1.1 A graphical depiction of the scrum framework with its workflow and key tools

How Change Became the Only Constant

The old platitude that change is the only constant has now become a worrisome fact that most businesses have to adjust to. Resting on old laurels and expecting customer loyalty have come to prove to be a proverbial death trap. Companies such as Blockbuster and Kodak are stark reminders of the fate that awaits corporates that are dominated by inertia and ignorance. It is becoming evident to most executives that they must learn to live with this uncertainty and find a framework that allows their businesses to embrace and thrive on it, or at least not be succumbed by it.

But How Did We Get to This Point?

We have come a long way since the industrial era and standardization of products offered with a "take it or leave it" approach. Consumerism in the digital economy is instead focused on individualization of goods and services to an extent never seen before, all underpinned by an accelerating pace of technical innovation. This is putting corporations under an enormous pressure to at all times make sure that their offerings are alluring and competitively priced. Marketing campaigns can now only do so much to rescue a dying brand whose products have become outdated, being a thing of the past with potentially only nostalgic value. And it is quickly moving beyond just manufacturing; the high-end service sector that up till recently had been little impacted by automation and digitalization efforts is now being hit with full force. What all this is adding up to are that corporations and employees alike will have to learn how to live in volatile markets. They must, in the true sense of the word, become agile to survive so that they quickly can respond and adapt to an evolving business environment. It means, to always be ready to deliver greater value in every area of the organization and hopefully reap the commercial benefits rather than face extinction. If customers cannot get the products and services they expect, they will simply go somewhere else; it is only a click away. Customers rightfully demand and expect that businesses will be able to rapidly change in order to meet their needs. Being big is no longer beautiful in many industries, in fact smaller players and start-ups often benefit from not having built up costly bureaucracies. This as scaling up not so much any longer depends on expanding manpower, as digitalization efforts by-and-large can easily produce more volume.

The agile methodology has proven from the project management perspective to provide a capable framework to deal with change. Might it also be applicable at the organizational level?

Endnotes

1. D. Nelson. 1970. *Frederick W. Taylor and the Rise of Scientific Management* (Madison: MIT Press).
2. A.E. Musson and E. Robinson. 1969. *Science and Technology in the Industrial Revolution* (Toronto, ON: University of Toronto Press).

3. Iacocca Institute. 1991. *21st Century Manufacturing Enterprise Strategy: An Industry Led View* (Bethlehem, PA: Iacocca Institute, Lehigh University).

4. G. Lee and W. Xia. 2010. "Toward Agile: An Integrated Analysis of Quantitative and Qualitative Field Data on Software Development Agility," *MIS Quarterly* 34, no. 1, pp. 87-114.

5. K. Beck, J. Grenning, R.C. Martin, M. Beedle, J. Highsmith, S. Mellor, A. van Bennekum, A. Hunt, K. Schwaber, A. Cockburnx, R. Jeffries, J. Sutherland, W. Cunningham, J. Kern, D. Thomas, M. Fowler, and B. Marick. 2001. *Manifesto for Agile Software Development* (Agile Alliance).

6. K. Beck, J. Grenning, R.C. Martin, M. Beedle, J. Highsmith, S. Mellor, A. van Bennekum, A. Hunt, K. Schwaber, A. Cockburn, R. Jeffries, J. Sutherland, W. Cunningham, J. Kern, D. Thomas, M. Fowler, and B. Marick. 2001. *Principles behind the Agile Manifesto* (Agile Alliance).

7. A. Moran. 2014. *Agile Risk Management* (Cham: Springer Verlag, SpringerBriefs in Computer Science).

8. K. Beck, J. Grenning, R.C. Martin, M. Beedle, J. Highsmith, S. Mellor, A. van Bennekum, A. Hunt, K. Schwaber, A. Cockburn, R. Jeffries, J. Sutherland, W. Cunningham, J. Kern, D. Thomas, M. Fowler, and B. Marick. 2001. *Principles behind the Agile Manifesto* (Agile Alliance).

9. B. Boehm and R. Turner. 2004. *Balancing Agility and Discipline: A Guide for the Perplexed* (Boston, MA: Addison-Wesley).

10. K. Beck, J. Grenning, R.C. Martin, M. Beedle, J. Highsmith, S. Mellor, A. van Bennekum, A. Hunt, K. Schwaber, A. Cockburn, R. Jeffries, J. Sutherland, W. Cunningham, J. Kern, D. Thomas, M. Fowler, and B. Marick. 2001. *Principles behind the Agile Manifesto* (Agile Alliance).

11. K. Beck and C. Andres. 2004. *Extreme Programming Explained: Embrace Change.* 2nd ed., (The XP Series) (Boston, MA: Addison-Wesley).

12. S. Ashmore and K. Runyan. 2014. *Introduction to Agile Methods* (Boston, MA: Addison-Wesley).

13. A. Moran. 2015. *Managing Agile: Strategy, Implementation, Organisation and People* (Cham: Springer Verlag).

14. K. Rubin. 2013. *Essential Scrum. A Practical Guide to the Most Popular Agile Process* (Boston, MA: Addison-Wesley).

15. K. Schwaber. 2004. *Agile Project Management with Scrum* (Washington, DC: Microsoft Press, Developer Best Practices).

16. G. Verheyen. 2013. *Scrum: A Pocket Guide (A Smart Travel Companion)* (Zaltbommel: Van Haren Publishing, Best Practice).

17. P. Deemer, G. Benefield, C. Larman, and B. Vodde. 17 December 2012. "The Scrum Primer: A Lightweight Guide to the Theory and Practice of Scrum," (Version 2.0), InfoQ. https://www.infoq.com/minibooks/Scrum_Primer/ (accessed 1 June 2020).

18. R. Pichler. 2010. *Agile Product Management with Scrum: Creating Products that Customers Love* (Upper Saddle River, NJ: Addison-Wesley).

19. P. Deemer, G. Benefield, C. Larman, and B. Vodde. 17 December 2012. "The Scrum Primer: A Lightweight Guide to the Theory and Practice of Scrum," (Version 2.0), InfoQ. https://www.infoq.com/minibooks/Scrum_Primer/ (accessed 1 June 2020).

20. K. Rubin. 2013. *Essential Scrum. A Practical Guide to the Most Popular Agile Process* (Boston, MA: Addison-Wesley).

CHAPTER 2

Agile and Then Some More Agile

Без революционной теории не может быть
революционного движения
*(Without revolutionary theory there can be no revolutionary
movement)*
—Vladimir Ilyich Ulyanov,
a.k.a. Lenin, Russian revolutionary (1870 to 1924)

Nowadays, few doubt that the changes that the digital economy brings with it will for most businesses mean an unusually uncertain future. Businesses will never really be sure of the commercial expiry dates of their products and services, as the technical innovation that is going to pull the carpet from under their feet is always looming. But will it be next week or perhaps next year? It is an environment that requires a constant vigilance and tools adapted to handle these never-ending uncertainties. The influencing trends in our digital economy extend far beyond technological paradigm shifts and upgrades, also including:

- An accelerating pace of demands and requests from customers, investors, even regulators, requiring new and better services, constant growth, and regulatory compliance, respectively;
- Unstable political and cultural trends where sometimes corporate and universal principles that are applied in certain markets are for business reasons neglected in others, even openly rejected (read: human rights in China), causing cognitive dissonance and moral decay;
- Constant introduction of new disruptive technologies. Established businesses and industries are being commoditized or replaced

through automation, including robotics and machine learning. In effect, many aspects of human input are becoming a thing of the past in many corporate functions;

- Accelerating digital transformations and democratization of information. The increased volumes, transparency, and distribution of information require organizations to rapidly engage in multidirectional communication tools and complex collaboration with stakeholders, including existing and potential customers; and

- Finding the right employees. The cognitive bar to join the digital economy has increased dramatically versus the now decaying industrial economy. The traditional factories and plants could pick up pretty much anyone from the street and with some rudimentary training they could quickly become a productive employee. Not so anymore. The ongoing digital transformations will in effect exclude large groups of the population from entering the labor market, other than in shorter stints as much as the economic cycle allows. It is something that is going to have severe societal consequences. Remarkably, this does not mean that corporates can freely choose when seeking to hire digital experts. Au contraire, for individual corporations, finding the value-add high cognitive employees is becoming increasingly difficult. The demand for truly gifted individuals, capable of lateral thinking and creativity, has probably never been higher. And they are not only competing with other firms to attract them. The start-up scene is vibrant and rarely has it been easier to go it alone, not much capital or equipment is needed—a good idea and a laptop are pretty much all it takes. Corporates will need to adapt their recruitment strategies, such as through bespoke selection programs and remunerations as well as continuous knowledge and learning transfers. They will have to get used to fast-track high-potential employees through the ranks and dismiss nonperformers in a much quicker pace than ever before. The quest to retain the best talent is now more than ever business critical and what is most highly sought after are individuals with the rather rare ability to innovate.

These trends are forcing corporations to organize themselves differently than the corporations of the past. But how?

Ensuring that the organization stays nimble and flexible is the prescribed remedy that is being promoted by business gurus. However, for a large corporation, these buzzwords often appear as contradictions of how by necessity it must conduct its operations. While these are admirable aspirations, realities on the ground generally make it unreachable ambitions. Traditionally, corporations organize themselves around products and services that, once launched, historically needed only relatively rare upgrades, this as the release of a completely new suite of products took years to come to fruition. Hence, in such a sterile environment, processes were highly specific, predictable, and could be developed through meticulous planning. The ones that planned best usually won, as it allowed them to become the most cost-efficient and provided them with the highest profit margins. Given the almost static nature of the manufacturing processes, an authoritarian management style operating on "command and control" was what worked best. The typical career path followed this hierarchical structure, with most of the power residing at the top of the pyramid. Employees were expected to spend their whole careers at the same firm, many focused on climbing the corporate ladder. By its very design, it created an oversized cadre of often very powerful middle managers that only really could expand their power base by building fiefdoms with bloated bureaucracies. These, however, were almost never that beneficial to the corporation at large. Many are the stories from corporate folklore of how poorly performing middle managers crafted ways to hide within the bureaucracy, circumventing any accountability, in the end becoming experts of doing nothing. Albeit rigid and slow moving, the benefits of this pyramid-shaped managerial structure were that it was strong and robust, and once executive directives had been broadcasted, the whole organization moved as a united force in the desired direction. But those days are now quickly coming to an end, the increased pace of pretty much everything is forcing a change in mindset and behavior, and the work-shy bureaucrats inside the corporations have started to sense their demise.

With agile having performed well at the project level, it has enticed senior management to study whether it could also be implemented across the organization, front-to-back. Agile properly adopted compels organizations to constantly assess their status quo, as it seeks to confront inefficiencies and adapt to changes instantly in order to secure long-term survival and success.

Therefore, the ultimate purpose of an agile organization is to embrace learning and accept improvement as a never-ending challenge. This by quickly implementing and commercializing new technologies, introducing more dynamic work arrangements by minimizing any cumbersome bureaucracy, all directed with a view to meet arbitrary customer needs. Agile is about providing the organization with the flexibility and ability to rapidly adapt and making sure that it steers itself on a commercially endurable and viable path. But to maintain the integrity of the organization, it must find the appropriate mix between this flexibility and stability. Trying to convert a large organization to a gigantic start-up of sorts, or a portfolio of projects perpetually commencing and concluding, will simply not be a viable solution for the long term. With no common distinctions holding it together, important features such as loyalty will wither away. The constant rearrangements of practices will have many employees start to question what their role in the organization really is and what can be expected. Hence, the challenge is to at all times both keep considering the reconfigurations of strategy, structure, processes, people, and technology toward value-creating opportunities and at the same time uphold some sort of stability. This is so as not to constantly keep the organization and its employees in limbo. Management consultants have been quick to jump on the agile bandwagon, pitching it with mouth-watering benefits that promise to solve the conundrums that organizations are facing. What are then the advantages that an agile organization is supposed to bring with it?

It operates by a strategy that spurs action rather than flaunting the fashionable but empty buzzwords

- The management should strive to make sure that the daily work and its outcomes are measurably connected to the strategy.
- Management through frequent feedback and ongoing coaching empowers employees with a certain independence and autonomy to find pragmatic means to achieve the outlined strategy.
- There is a continuous orientation toward performance with the contributions of individual employees and teams alike evaluated by cross-functional business metrics and targets.
- The strategy is instilled as a guiding beacon among employees who are encouraged to contribute to its formulation. It should

be crafted so as to prompt a feeling of being both professionally and emotionally invested in the work as well as foster team spirit through a shared destiny.

The business architecture is purposely arranged to promote action

- The decision-making power is as far as possible delegated to the employees closest to the action, and they are given authority to influence development and implementation of solutions.
- The leadership emphasizes teamwork and encourages employees to also engage in strategic and organizational decisions with a view to create a community spirit. Coaching is a pivotal tool in this leadership model, aspiring to reduce the traditional authoritarian hierarchy to a minimum.
- The organization enables employees to work in small, self-managing teams accountable for the end-to-end work of a specific product or service, and these are formed and demobilized accordingly.
- Promotions and career paths are focused on performance and quality achievements rather than years of service and office politics. Moving up the career ladder in the agile organization should depend on merits alone. This provides a highly dynamic feature in how roles and responsibilities are allotted.
- There is the creation of an ecosystem that reaches beyond the boundaries of the organization, including customers, vendors, and other partners seeking to cojointly develop new products and services. These arrangements with external parties are tailored and flexible to make sure that productivity and profitability are optimized.

An entrepreneurial spirit is encouraged and formalized

- The agile organization seeks to become a body on a constant quest of identifying and seizing commercial opportunities and ensuring that it remains flexible enough to adequately resource them. There is a systematic and rapid process in place, such as a new business committee, to regularly evaluate and decide on new business initiatives. If getting a go ahead, cross-functional teams of business and technology employees can quickly be deployed to act on the perceived opportunities. The technological infrastructure is nimble enough to allow for the integration of new products and services. To facilitate this objective, modular architecture is used, technology is updated in shorter intervals of time, and automated testing enables continuous releases of software.

- Entrepreneurship thrives on creative experimentation aspiring to seek out new ways of doing things and introducing new products and services. Employees are provided open access to unfiltered data on products, customers, and market data with forums to share ideas and results from testing and the development of prototypes. In all, the agile organization seeks to provide an encouraging and fertile environment for innovation.

- Continuous learning enhances employees' knowledge base as well as boosts the organizational cognitive capital. It especially takes aim at making sure that the educational efforts are means to improve business processes and better understand markets. The learning process is facilitated through bespoke tools and structured processes, integrated into the day-to-day workflow.[1,2]

So, to arrive at these advantages, what are the transformational steps to establish an agile organization?

A multipronged approach is needed, where a lot of emphasis is put on soft values such as corporate culture, and senior sponsors are expected to fully live the act and stay committed to the agile philosophy. Organizationally, the transformation seeks to remove as much as possible of the managerial hierarchy and instead install networks of teams that work closer to the markets. It is typically done through commencing pilots, which are rolled out in a step-by-step mode where business functions deemed most suitable to the agile format act as role models for the ensuing implementation efforts. The agile teams, through the network formation, are arranged as projects, consisting of employees selected for their adequate, often well-rounded, skillsets. The roles rather than being fixed are of a temporary nature, only existing until the specific projects are concluded. Job descriptions are therefore more elusive, with employees being expected to move around in interim arrangements, solely depending on their competences and performance rather than being manipulated by office politics. With the senior leadership seeking to flatten out the hierarchy, traditional career paths become increasingly rarer. It in effect means that the role of the middle manager comes under threat as their positions no longer really serve a purpose in the agile organization. And it is when this insight becomes apparent to the middle managers that the problems usually start.[3,4]

With the Promises of Such Alluring Benefits, What Could Possibly Go Wrong?

Despite the many acclaimed benefits that a transformation to an agile organization will provide, according to diehard *agilistas* at least, there are very few real-world showcases of corporations of size claiming to truly be agile throughout. When the first enthusiasm has faded, if it even was there in the first place, many of the business functions tend to fall back to previous work practices, and the SAFe certification diplomas, or similar, become nothing more than ornaments on office walls.

The agile philosophy has proven to work very well in a turbulent environment where one is not only expected to face disruptions but actually proactively generate it. From that perspective, agile has also to some extent become synonymous with creativity and innovation. But that kind of disruption is what some corporate functions fear the most, and for good reasons, executives are not hiring compliance officers, accountants, and HR specialists to be mavericks, instead a risk-averse personality is what is sought after. The very thought of an employee with an agile mindset among them constantly trying to "improve" processes will make them highly uneasy. This is recognized but rarely articulated, and many rollouts of agile frameworks into organizations make of point of conducting a phased approach where certain functions in practice, while not in theory, are basically omitted. Of course, no one pretended that transforming one's corporation from the traditional hierarchical model to an agile operating model was ever going to be easy. Cultural chocks among employees when they realize that there is more to this than the usual consulting gimmicks, in some cases severe such, are not an unusual reaction.

Breaking down a static, siloed, structural hierarchy and moving to a network of teams operating in rapid learning and decision-making cycles is indeed a massive undertaking, which will shake the very core of the organization. A key feature of the resistance to the agile organization might be that it is a much more high-energy venture than the traditional corporation. Everything is expected to be speeded up with a focus on getting things done, all this highly concerning to the bureaucratic cadre of the organization, marinated in doing things by the book (slowly), and if the book is constantly being rewritten, opposition is bound to occur. It is however rarely made public and turned into open rebellion. This is because agile has become such a strong buzzword that it is on every executive's lips over the past decade, thus any vocal resistance, even fierce but fair critique, comes with the risk of being a career-ending move. So, everyone will endorse it, but apart from the relatively few zealous agile proponents, typically with an IT background from where they can testify to the good results, most employees will remain lukewarm at best. An organizational transformation of this drastic nature brings with it a lot of stress, including an insight that the agile framework in particular takes aim at middle managers. And when they realize that they are facing a highly uncertain future, something always glossed over by the agile sponsors, a troublesome realization will dawn on many. Namely that what the agile organization supposedly brings with it is that employees to a greater degree than before will be held accountable, even on a daily basis. They are expected to work harder and faster. For promotions, long years of service will account for little, being able to deliver is what counts, in particular doing it with a technical flair. But middle managers are often more powerful than what their corporate rank might allude, they have extensive both horizontal and vertical networks. They can have influencing powers in strategic corporate decisions, albeit mostly informally as power brokers. Middle managers tend to have served a long time at the firm and their loyalty is beyond doubt. They know all nooks and crannies within the organization, which levers to pull when they need to get something done; however, they are typically too busy protecting their fiefdoms than doing much else. If they feel that their powerbase is threatened, they constitute formidable opponents capable of putting an effective stop to any strategic initiative, mostly through covert acts. By deliberate passivity, they make sure projects go stale, eventually withering away, something which many sponsors of agile organization transformations have come to experience. The point of contention is the aspiration of the agile philosophy to eliminate as much as is viable of the bureaucracy, which provides many middle managers with influence and justifies their very reason to exist. In many large corporations, the middle management ranks often have quite fudged responsibilities, seldom any obligations to actually deliver anything tangible and value-added, and no clear measurable metrics of performance. Much of their workdays are spent in committees or similar, preparing endless amounts of documents. They generally are too detached from customer relationships or product development and therefore lack the in-depth skills to discuss matters in detail. Hence, they can make few actual decisions over items that truly matter, instead trying to justify themselves by standing on ceremony. This governance structure is declared to act as a risk management mechanism, being part of the three lines of defense. However, as the involved sit too far from the actual work and markets, they lack the skills, in particular technical skills, or the diligence to understand what the exposed risks might actually be and how to mitigate them. But the solution is not to fire them en masse, their role in certain functions is still pivotal. Bureaucracies seem to form even in technological start-ups that have grown into large size corporations, such as their Accounting, Compliance, Finance, Legal, and HR functions, which are rarely more agile and automated than those of corporations from the old economy. Interestingly, they tend to recruit the same type of risk-averse personalities for these functions as any other firms. For these control-focused units, still much is needed and required for regulatory reasons; hierarchical structures with standardized process are generally the best method we have to organize such type of work. Many bureaucracies have developed a lot of silent knowledge that cannot be easily replaced nor automated. The staff turnover in these functions tends to be a lot lower than in the business, meaning that these employees have developed better informal networks throughout the firm and take a longer term view of their careers. This goes hand in hand with their loyalty toward the firm of which they often are being praised for, and rightfully so, perhaps this is the main characteristic of a long-serving middle manager. They have stuck with the firm in thick and thin, been perfect corporate citizens, such as often being engaged in charities. But does one thing, by necessity, exclude another, cannot these bureaucrats be rewired, embracing change instead of shunning it? A pondering that brings us to what is agile's perhaps most contentious issue: is there an innate agile mindset? It means that if you do not have it, there is little any amount of training can do to make you agile, as you simply do not have it in you. If this is the case, does the stereotypical average middle manager entrenched in corporate red tape lack it? When one ask the consulting services selling agile implementations, their default answer is that anyone can be agile. That, however, might be an answer more motivated by vested commercial interests rather than any in-depth research or actual experiences on the ground backing this unequivocal statement. Given the popularity of agile methodologies now spanning over almost two decades, there is surprisingly little research on the psychological traits beneficial to prosper in an environment dominated by its work practices. It is testified to be highly intense and energy draining; it certainly requires a capacity to deal with the stress stemming from the uncertainties it evokes. Ideally, it also requires a creative capability to find new solutions to problems. Stress, a pressure to constantly perform and being judged by its deliverables, and no clear guidelines on what the next steps might be—these certainly do not sound like a workplace that many would feel comfortable in, let alone be able to excel in; rather, it is an environment most would seek to actively avoid, even undermine if given a chance. When studying what is needed to succeed in an agile setting, it comes close to equate the entrepreneurial mindset. Two of the key characteristics are a willingness to embrace risk and a cognitive capability to make sure these are calculated risks rather than just recklessly throwing oneself into the unknown. Both of these are relatively strongly influenced by hereditary factors. So, if you have not got the genetics on your side, it is hard for any type of training to rewire your mind to become agile. Hence, what is required is to be a risk taker rather than be risk averse, thrive in uncertainty, prone to action rather than too meticulous planning, with an impatience to execute and a rebellious streak that questions authority. In all, factors that have proven difficult to be permanently altered: educational effects will relatively quickly be abating with individuals returning to their default personality settings. Of course, these characteristics must be viewed in a relative rather than absolute degree.

Herein lies the likely answer to why we are seeing so few corporations fully embrace the agile methodology as a firmwide organizational structure, amongst its employees only a minority are likely to be equipped with an agile mindset. Instead, the pragmatic solution is to allow for a delineation between the front-office vis-à-vis the back-office functions of the organization. Something that is proving not to be entirely synchronized, with conflicting managerial models leading to clashes at interfacing points. So, if we are going to have to live with this organizational model for the time being, how can we then make sure that the business is optimized for innovation, and as little as possible distracted by red tape and institutional dysfunctions? The features of the innovating organization might be the answer.[5-12]

Endnotes

1. E. Sherina, K. Krish, and T. Shail. October 2018. "Harnessing Agile Compendium," McKinsey & Company. https://www.mckinsey .com/~/media/McKinsey/Business%20Functions/Organization/ Our%20Insights/Harnessing%20agile%20compendium/Harnessing-Agile-compendium-October-2018.ashx (accessed 1 June 2020).

2. K. Christian, B. Lars, S. Thorsten, V. Marcus, B. Thole, L. Christian, and R. Richarda. August 2017. "Agile Organizations: An Approach for a Successful Journey towards More Agility in Daily Business," Capgemini Consulting. https://www.capgemini.com/consulting-de/wp-content/uploads/sites/32/2017/08/cc_agile_organization_ pov_20170508.pdf (accessed 1 June 2020).

3. B. Daniel, E. Sherina, H. Christopher, and T. Shail. May 2019. "The Journey to an Agile Organization," McKinsey & Company. https:// www.mckinsey.com/business-functions/organization/our-insights/ the-journey-to-an-agile-organization (accessed 1 June 2020).

4. K. Christian, B. Lars, S. Thorsten, V. Marcus, B. Thole, L. Christian, and R. Richarda. August 2017. "Agile Organizations: An Approach for a Successful Journey towards More Agility in Daily Business," Capgemini Consulting. https://www.capgemini.com/consulting-de/wp-content/uploads/sites/32/2017/08/cc_agile_organization_ pov_20170508.pdf (accessed 1 June 2020).

5. D.K. Rigby, J. Sutherland, and H. Takeuchi. May 2016. "Embracing Agile," Harvard Business Review. https://hbr.org/2016/05/embracing-agile (accessed 1 June 2020).

6. L. Gren. 2015. "Using the Work and Organizational Psychology Perspective in Research on Agile Software Development Teams," Computer Science. https://www.semanticscholar.org/paper/Using-the-Work-and-Organizational-Psychology-in-on-Gren/8634c226690fe73f0ee891f0e2d35a140a6f38e4 (accessed 1 June 2020).

7. T. Sara and C. Elin. 2019. "The Role of Psychological Safety in Implementing Agile Methods across Cultures," *Research-Technology Management* 62, no. 2. https://www.tandfonline.com/doi/full/10.1080/08956308.2019.1563436 (accessed 1 June 2020).

8. C. James and F. Shelli. *The Psychology of Agile Team Leadership* (Chapter in Agile Project Management: Managing for Success), pp. 9-25.

9. N. Nicolaou and S. Shane. 2019. "Common Genetic Effects on Risk-taking Preferences and Choices," *Journal of Risk and Uncertainty* 59, pp. 261-79. https://link.springer.com/article/10.1007/s11166-019-09316-2 (accessed 1 June 2020).

10. N. Nicolaou and S. Shane. 2010. "Entrepreneurship and Occupational Choice: Genetic and Environmental Influences," *Journal of Economic Behavior & Organization* 76, pp. 3-14.

11. L.L. Rao, Y. Zhou, D. Zheng, L.Q. Yang, and S. Li. 1 October 2018. "Genetic Contribution to Variation in Risk Taking: A Functional MRI Twin Study of the Balloon Analogue Risk Task," *Psychological Science* 29, no. 10, pp. 1679-91. https://journals.sagepub.com/doi/10.1177/0956797618779961 (accessed 1 June 2020).

12. R.P. Ebstein, J. Benjamin, and R.H. Belmaker. 2003. "Behavioral Genetics, Genomics, and Personality." In *Behavioral Genetics in the Postgenomic Era,* ed. R. Plomin, J.C. DeFries, I.W. Craig, and P. McGuffin. Washington, DC: American Psychological Association.

CHAPTER 3

The Innovating Organization

Man muss noch Chaos in sich haben, um einen tanzenden Stern
gebären zu können
(You must have chaos within you to give birth to a dancing star)
—Friedrich Nietzsche, German philosopher (1844 to 1900)

The attempts to introduce a full-scale agile organization have largely come to nought owing to a failure, or perhaps a refusal, to recognize that operating by an agile mindset is ill-suited to some corporate functions. These include the various types of controls and policing of ongoing operations from accounting and compliance with laws and regulations to the traditional responsibilities of human resources. In these units, stability of processes and people are key principles to live by and are best arranged through a hierarchy to ensure consistency. Therefore, a delineation of the organization makes sense for want of better organizational arrangements. Hence, it means accepting a differentiation between bureaucratic units with their standardized processes seeing relatively little change being managed by risk-averse employees and business units where change is what one lives by. There, an agile mindset will serve as a useful perspective to accommodate and, as far as possible, leverage the opportunities that arise from instigating change. These business units will share similarities with start-ups both in culture and dynamic processes, and their sole reason for commercially existing will be to provide the market with products and service that customers, directly or indirectly, are willing to pay for. To achieve this, innovation is a key feature, and the corporations most adapted to produce value-added innovations, both as internal efforts as well as utilizing independent initiatives, are likely to come out as winners. But how does innovation happen and how does one organize oneself to embrace an innovative culture?

History provides us with the insight that human advances often happen through innovative jumps. Quantum leap technology elevates mankind, whether that be the discovery of fire, applying wheels for transportation, or splitting of atoms, space travel, and beyond. Of the former we know little of the creative process, whereas of the latter we know a lot, at least at the superficial level. According to legend, it was when the Greek universal genius Archimedes stepped into the bathtub and noticed how the water level rose that he experienced a sudden insight into calculating volume and proclaimed *Eureka!* (I have found it!). Similarly, a falling apple provided the cue to English physicist Isaac Newton, who then formulated the laws of gravity. German-American physicist Albert Einstein's imaginary vision of riding on a beam of light played a significant role in his development of the general theory of relativity. Although some of these historical accounts are claimed to be fictitious, at least in part, the phenomena they highlight are not.

The process of creativity has been closely linked to these eureka moments: sudden cognitive breakthroughs, relatively rare, that unfold a perspective not thought of earlier and that provide annotative knowledge surpassing the existing scientific doctrine. Sometimes, it carries the traits of the aforementioned sudden revelation of sorts, whereas at other times it is part of a more gradual process where the levels of insight advance step by step. Thinking outside the box plays an important role as part of the ability to view the world differently than contemporary scientists. But not just in a random manner. This is also a madman's worldview that differs from the normative perspective, yet he does not manage to proceed beyond disarray. What sets the innovative thinker apart is that what appears to be a chaotic chasm in the process of creativity to the layman is where he, through a structured process, albeit the innovator himself generally is at pains to explain it, often manages to produce new valuable knowledge. The truly innovative manage to bring order out of the chaotic that delivers a new insight and augments our understanding of certain phenomena. American philosopher of science Thomas Kuhn (1922 to 1996), in his book *The Structure of Scientific Revolutions* (1962), suggested that scientific knowledge, rather than following a path of linear progress, advances through infrequent spurts of knowledge jumps, or paradigm shifts. These thereby render the existing thought narrative obsolete, as its perspective on reality was too limited. The new set of knowledge is eventually being recognized as a scientific truth by the research community. There is obviously a subjective element in this acknowledgment, but it will establish the axioms that dictate the future interpretation of scientific findings.[1]

There has been extensive research on how this creative process works and what its main steps are, which is not surprising given the potential commercial and scientific values that cracking the code of creativity holds. Interestingly, one of the earliest writings on the creative process, dating back almost a century, still represent the dominant hypothesis. English psychologist Graham Wallas (1858 to 1932), in his book, *The Art of Thought* (1926), identified four stages of creativity:

  I. Preparation;
 II. Incubation;
III. Illumination; and,
 IV. Verification.[2]

As part of the preparation phase, the problem, or issue at hand, is detailed and defined, and the data and information required are collated and categorized. The background material is analyzed and a knowledge base accumulated. The preparatory phase also entails the planning of the project.

Unlike the preparation phase, which is consciously active and deliberate, the incubation phase is one where much of the problem-solving activity is conducted unconsciously. This is in a sense the most mysterious part of the whole process, where the conscious consideration of the problem is replaced, if a viable solution cannot be identified, by unconscious contemplation in which Boolean logic is relaxed and association-based thought processes, also of the bizarre kind, are engaged. In Wallas' own words,

> Voluntary abstention from conscious thought on any problem may, itself, take two forms: the period of abstention may be spent either in conscious mental work on other problems, or in a relaxation from all conscious mental work. The first kind of Incubation economizes time, and is therefore often the better.[3]

This incubation phase often comes with a great deal of frustration and anxiety, in that a large number of proposed ideas usually prove futile. The emotional stress that builds up brings unconscious mental processes under further duress. Obviously, a lot of research projects end at the incubation phase, as they fail to find a workable solution. But in some instances, the eureka moment appears, and a creative idea arises out of chaos. The incubation phase has been described as the characteristics of the problem being hypothesized into an abstract mental representation that are then tweaked, distorted, and rearranged in various ways, in the aspiration to identify a solution.[4]

The arrival at the solution represents the third phase of Wallas' model, the illumination phase. It cannot directly be consciously forced or provoked to a conclusion but is largely dictated by an individual's ability to form variations of the mental model representing the problem. The illumination phase has puzzled many researchers on creativity, and, according to most theories, this decisive part of the creative breakthrough often emanates from the unconscious. The question then arises, what is it in the unconscious that occurs that the conscious sometimes are not capable of doing?

French mathematician Henri Poincaré (1854 to 1912) was among the first to explicitly write about an unconsciously driven idea- and solution generating process, and his focus, quite naturally, was on mathematical creativity. He argued that trial and error played a key part in creativity, generating random scenarios that contained various associations of ideas and elements that at times could give rise to solutions. However, given the almost infinite numbers of scenarios that can be conceived, how is the selection of potentially useful ones conducted, and how are these brought forward to our conscious awareness for contemplation and evaluation? Poincaré argued that they had to be felt, meaning that a feeling arises that somehow harmonizes and provides an insight into the conclusion. From the intellectual point of view, it must hold an aesthetic value. The solution is identified through expert insight of the domain area in question so that a mathematician like himself would identify and feel the elegant quality of the proposed mathematical solution, whereas that would not appear obvious to a nonmathematician.[5] What more recent research proposes is that it appears that the unconscious somehow organizes information in a better way than conscious thought patterns do and manages to decoct it into a more focus-based perspective through some sort of filtering mechanism. It is not as restricted by narrative constraints that put blinders on our deliberate reasoning and therefore allows for a more free-flowing form of association-based thinking. The unconscious operates through a form of automatic spreading activation along associative links, where connecting chains actively seek out unusual yet productive combinations. It also suggests that the unconscious holds the capability to process disorganized and incomplete information and has the ability to do so until it evolves into a better and better form of a mental model representing a possible solution. This means reaching some sort of equilibrium, or goal, that provides a signal to transfer the results thereof to the conscious part of the mind.[6,7] However, the aesthetic aspect of a creative solution as that proposed by Poincaré, and others after him, comes with interesting insights; it means that it can then be formulated as symmetry seeking formulae and might thereby be possible to automate.

Thus, once a solution has emerged, it needs validation. This is done by formulating the often highly symbolic insights into proper prose and mathematics, much like Einstein transformed his vision of riding a lightning beam into the general theory of relativity. This manifestation and documentation represent the verification phase. Following Wallas' theory, a number of theories on the process of creativity have evolved that, by and large, follow a similar evolution, with the moment of illumination still being the least understood part.

But Can Anyone Be Creative?

Creativity that manifests in innovative commercial and scientific achievements, and the great arts, seems bestowed only on a few. It appears that creativity, of such a highly abstract caliber, must be viewed as an add-on to what can be defined as "normal" human thought patterns. This is an acknowledgment that a considerable number of innovations originate from the so-called lonely genius, characterized by a combination of obsessively hard work, the courage to see things through against the reigning normative convictions, with the ability to view the world through a different lens. Despite many attempts, innovation-through-committees is not really taking off, and recognizing the advantages that teamwork holds, it often cannot outmatch the lonely genius approach to creative, in particular transformative, innovation. Both the scientific and artistic fields are still dominated by the lonely genius types, as evidenced in the bestselling literature, art, and music, all being produced by individuals and not groups of authors, painters, or musicians working together. And, typically, the Nobel Prize in the various natural sciences is awarded to individuals rather than research teams.

Most researchers agree that a certain level of cognitive ability is necessary for creativity, including the capacity to make flexible associations between abstract thoughts as well as the capability and judgment to generate original ideas that are apt to solve the task at hand, as simply unusual ideas that are not useful or adaptive should not really be considered creative. But strong cognitive faculties are not enough for creativity, the latter also requiring a personality that is willing to confront conformity; in other words, a certain courageous, even rebellious, streak, and for this there needs to be a willingness to deal with great uncertainties, because it is typically associated with engaging in work lacking defined output, even paths to solutions, and thus involves considerable risk-taking, features known to motivate only certain individuals. And unsurprisingly, studies have revealed that individuals with an inherent curiosity tend to be more motivated to engage in creative work.[8–11]

How to Form Teams (or a Collective Intelligence) That Incite the Creative Process?

Of course, the failure rates in the innovative process will be high, possibly too high for result-driven executives, who might, after a succession of failures, decide to close down the venture. This would be because it faces so much uncertainties, not exactly knowing if and when there will be any tangible deliverables, making any realistic financial projections virtually impossible. It is therefore an open secret that many big corporations now only innovate in name, Apple being a case in point. They are often held down by the expectations of imminent financial results and an overwhelming bureaucracy with burdensome committee structures required to approve any new initiatives.

Altogether not a place for free spirits to engage in innovations that might transcend product lines and functions, even if budgets tend to be overly generous.

How can innovation be encouraged? In what type of environment does it thrive? What should an innovate team look like?

The one-of-a-kind innovator-cum-entrepreneur appears relatively infrequently, even if serious efforts have been made to groom and nurture them, and there is no dearth of entrepreneurship programs at various levels. Some of them become one-hit wonders, most of them fail to take off at all, and some have an independent streak and decide to strike out on their own, establishing start-ups. But even if found working for a corporation, they tend only occasionally to receive the support and recognition they need to be successful. This is because some of their ideas will stand out as being too advanced and seemingly too detached for conventional thinking and are then rejected by less creative, and sometimes jealous, colleagues. However, it is around such personalities, as available, that businesses need to develop, basically forming a type of in-house start-ups, highly ad hoc in nature, and prepared to constantly shift focus. Thus, it is an environment both exceptionally unstable and unpredictable, but if and when ideas form into prototypes and eventually products, the process of standardization can begin, by handing it over to a more structured manufacturing process.

But what do you do, if you do not have this lonely genius innovator in your midst? Can this unique set of knowledge in various areas and thought patterns be replicated, so that instead a team can, in a consolidated manner, replicate these features? Broadly, two main ingredients are required in innovative work: domain expertise that relies on a well-organized knowledge base, much as the mathematician needs specific tools to solve mathematical problems, and a creative capability that facilitates the identification of potential solutions from among a variety of alternatives. Innovative creativity in that sense assumes a certain level of expertise. But relying on single-domain expertise alone also carries a danger, because in it lie tacit assumptions that can evolve into cognitive chains that are being taken for granted. These can become hard to intellectually detach oneself from as they serve as edificial axioms, as an innovative challenge needs to be considered from a variety of knowledge perspectives.

So what would the composition in a setup geared for innovation through a collective intelligence effort look like? There are some studies on the preferred makeup of teams that enhance creative capabilities. It is a blend of individuals that have these quirky, even eccentric and awkward, personalities with a proclivity for original thinking and drive and intellectual curiosity to solve problems, paired with individuals having the entrepreneurial can-do fixer characteristics. None of the team members need to match the cognitive capacity of "the lonely genius" but should share his personal characteristics. The original thinkers, often of an introvert nature, show their daring attitudes in exploring new ideas, sometimes in stark contrast to conventional thinking, which typically becomes the starting point. The entrepreneur type is good at organizing and practical problem-solving, whether that be finding financing, networks, or equipment. Both these types appear, implicitly at least, to proactively seek to be provocative and unorthodox, and at the same time embrace chaos and find pleasure in establishing some type of order in it. However, once a solution has been found and things go stale, they tend to quickly lose interest and get to work on the next thing that takes their fancy. This loss of interest can include difficulties and even a reluctance to document their results and establish a process to standardize them. In short, such a team is a blend of *the thinker* and *the doer,* with both types not afraid of cutting corners, but, if appropriately arranged, they are capable of delivering the (at times) improbable and value-adding ideas. The process of getting there not unusually includes overriding or breaking internal and external rules (and actually finding joy in doing so) through this zealous and gung ho attitude to prove a point and make things happen. As they are often seen as unconventional and also prone to breaking rules, they are at risk of causing controversy, even to the point of being dismissed. This can happen particularly in an organization that stands on ceremony, with its employees seeking to do everything by the book, and the innovative team will need senior sponsorship acting as guardian angels and taking them under their wing to protect them from harmful office politics.

What will the working environment in these teams be like? From numerous studies, some common denominators emerge: It is characterized by an open attitude, where anyone with new ideas is always welcome to present them with the assurance that they will receive serious

consideration. The team members, while endorsing the collective participation of the group, simultaneously show a great degree of independence,
rather than conforming to group thinking for the sake of it. This allows
individual perspectives to form a collective intelligence while still not ex-
cluding ambiguities, an important intellectual feature in that it preserves
a certain dynamism to remain open to alternative input. Another feature
of successful innovative teams is the focus on quality rather than quantity,
with proposed solutions being thoroughly dissected and reviewed from
all possible angles to identify potential deficiencies. This is regardless of
the rank of its proponent, which in another setting could be shielded
from criticism because of the pecking order. The selection process of team
members is harsh, and these groups are exceptionally elitist, accepting no
one deemed only good or below. Not surprisingly, these environments are
highly accommodating to risk, but only calculated risks, thereby forgiving
of mistakes, not by incompetence but by intelligent experimentation. It is
a convoluted setting with an openness to experimentation and creativity,
yet with a high degree of intolerance to incompetence and mediocracy.
So anyone with a lack of matching competence is likely to be ousted
quickly, given the intense focus on getting results. It is an environment
that will be highly unsuitable for many, because there is very little consen-
sual decision-making in a committee-like manner, as it is all about being
right. Thus, they are usually characterized by a brutal honesty, through an
open debate that holds no intellectual no-go zones with little room for
small talk, exchanging pleasantries and subtleties, and criticism, even if
harsh, becomes an aim to progress work. Through their highly selective
recruitment, the teams are often small, something that promotes intimate
and intense cooperation, void of any institutional predicaments. In all,
flexibility, an unbiased view of individuals but a highly biased view of the
quality of their work, and informality in terms of working arrangement
are the key concepts for organizations that have a documented record of
successful innovations. This is in stark contrast to the bureaucratic organizations seeking to control their employees' behavior in order to render
them reliable and predictable and skeptical of surprises, even positive ones,
which are, not unusually, deemed unfavorable for career advancements. A
more interesting observation is that many creative individuals appear geo-
graphically mobile, operating and doing most of their productive work

outside their native environments, obviously to various degrees and productivity not necessarily increasing with distance. But a certain multitude of thoughts and variation in cultural settings from those of one's formative years appear to stimulate creativity; not that any cultural mixture will augment creativity, however certain variations from too uniform and homogeneous settings are favorable. For a positive synergy to occur between these disparate personality types, a bespoke leadership is needed that can understand both their perspectives, focus, and, as required, channel rebellious tendencies in a constructive direction. This leader must also have the authority in terms of both knowledge and people leadership and a commercial acumen to eventually make sure that value-added products are delivered. To manage such groups is challenging given the often chaotic environment and the open-ended requirements to understand a problem. The many perspectives require an ability to cross-reference concepts from a multitude of subjects with an open mind. This is something traditional authoritarian leaders eager to fully control and even micromanage everything will struggle with, and that can lead to the ruin of a creative, albeit seemingly disorganized, atmosphere.[12,13]

Creativity Comes in Two Types…

One can distinguish between *primary* (sometimes labeled major) and *secondary* (or minor) creativity, where primary creativity represents something uniquely new, in effect a paradigm shift, and secondary creativity consists of innovative ways of applying an already known technology. Creativity researcher Margaret A. Boden distinguishes between three types of creativity: *combinational* (the unfamiliar combinations of familiar ideas); *exploratory* (exploring a conceptual space); and the most radical kind of creativity, *transformational* (transforming a conceptual space), the enabling of thoughts that have not been thought before.[14] Hence, there are different ways of characterizing creativity, and various proponents argue their type of classifications, but, broadly, they fall between the breakthrough paradigm shifting type and the enablement of existing methods in a new value-adding manner. Of course, the creative types one hold in-house will be decisive for where on the scale one's innovative efforts should aspire to be:

- Exploratory; typically, the bread and butter of teams focused on innovation. In terms of innovation, it is fairly low-level work and carries a higher probability of success, namely, by seeking variations of existing products and/or minor upgrades trying to develop new features as part of upgrades. Some of these modifications that hold commercial values might be identified through consumer surveys, and product variations might be possible through automated scenarios, thereby reducing reliance and freeing up key personnel for more challenging creative work.

- Combinational; testing out unfamiliar combinations of familiar ideas, such as adding unexpected but useful features to existing products. Divergent thinking techniques, such as brainstorming, can help to identify value-adding combinations. Guided combinations could, through automated generation of scenarios, be analyzed and tested out, in order to seek previously unthought-of combinations. The more unusual value-adding combinations can often be classified as belonging to the next more radical category.

- Transformational; Creative ideas with low probability but high value, typically characterized as being a break, often profound, from previous assumptions on how things are supposed to work. This means that by existing assumptions and theories, these transformational ideas cannot be deduced logically or through causality from the routine set of deployed inputs. Thus, it is a discontinuity of current practices. The transformational ideas often rest on a certain degree of serendipity, or some would say luck (or randomness) rather than deductive reasoning, and therefore by default the moment of enlightening becomes unpredictable and spontaneous. As previously noted, history has shown that there is a strong reliance on the lonely genius achieving previously unthought-of breakthroughs, which makes it difficult to fit within assigned project deadlines. Also, given the unpredictability of these transformational ideas, they might arise without any designated motivation preceding it; in other words, they might solve problems that are not part of the current strategy. They can therefore be said to be thinking without a specific goal, absent of either a fixed starting point or anticipated end product. Such transformational break-throughs lie outside the typical innovation framework, and agile methods can hardly facilitate or speed up what is largely an unconscious process.

Innovation in an Agile Context

Many can witness to how the adoption of an agile philosophy has helped to recast software development; its success has been noted in the improved quality and increased pace at which new applications are brought to the market by boosting the productivity of development teams. This was achieved by breaking down bureaucratic barriers and authoritarian hierarchies both psychologically and physically, and instead promoting self-organized and self-managed highly delivery-focused multidisciplinary teams working intimately together. More implicit perhaps, but no less important, was the change in mindset that the agile methodology fostered, and a leadership style that was more focused on coaching and empowering rather than dictating. So with the noted successes in software development, several questions arise, namely, can the agile method also be deployed to augment the generic creative process and help corporations deliver value-added innovations? Can it help employees become more creative? Can it remove the organizational impediments to encourage original thinkers that need a degree of freedom to excel in creativity? But creative thoughts are often transgressions and confrontations against the existing narrative, something that employees preferring routine and stability will find highly provocative and perceive as a threat to the existing order with comments like 'this is the way we have always done things', a practice far more common than even companies acclaimed as the most innovative like to admit. An agile methodology could ring-fence innovation zones providing that sort of controlled chaos that promotes the creativity that spurs innovation, and it can contextualize innovation so that it is considered from broader perspectives, not only as cutting-edge technology products and services, but also as continuous upgrades, as well as internal innovative ways of making the organization more efficient, and ultimately more profitable.[15] Some of these advantageous agile practices should include the following:

- Empower employees with the privilege to take the initiative to freely form teams to innovate within the strategic direction of the corporation, and formally endorse such ventures by granting them autonomy. Once a problem or prospective commercial idea has been identified in this bottom-up approach, senior management must encourage a self-forming team to establish itself, additionally motivated with performance-based remuneration upon successful deliverables, and ensure time and space for them to begin the work. They must be equipped with the flexibility to work on these projects aside from their line role's responsibilities.

- Work closely with the customer segments one seeks to target to reduce the risk of misalignment with their actual needs. The agile methodology has highlighted that this is best achieved through small-scale projects with the development teams embedded with customers, seeking input and ensuring open channels that provide feedback as quickly as possible. And an important principle is that what the customers say must precede the viewpoints of internal bureaucracy, such as when it comes to organizational alignments by products or services.

- Conduct continuous retrospectives to ensure a focus on enhancements and subsequent upgrades. Such an endeavor can be made possible only by fostering a no-blame culture, where experiments with product developments, even unorthodox ones, are encouraged. However, only a leader with a genuine agile mindset is geared to handle the many mistakes likely to be produced in the initial phase of the project. The uncertainty of what direction the product development will take brings with it considerable stress and might be challenged by senior management as wasting valuable time. It will also require a determined focus and an iron-fist approach to, at all times, prioritizing and reprioritizing proposals and ideas to ensure that the project can produce tangible deliverables.

- The teams tend to work best if structured vertically rather than horizontally, this to enable each team to be responsible for a complete application. It facilitates a holistic view of the functionality at all layers, with the domain experts extending their inputs beyond just crafting the underlying blueprint and logic of the functionalities, and hence the design–development–testing iterative loop becomes extended and embedded in the project work.

- Encourage fluid roles and responsibilities to enable the concept of cross-functional teams. Because the teams are of a temporary nature, put together solely for the duration of the development project, there is no need to restructure the corporation for particular projects on a permanent basis. This as the product development becomes an integral part of corporate life with constantly ongoing temporary and highly dynamic setups of development teams starting and concluding projects. To promote the agile organization and its philosophy, employees showing outstanding performance, arising from creative ability and a "can-do" spirit in these ventures, are culled for a fast-lane career track to develop internal role models.

- Introduce an open door policy. Senior management must allow employees to talk directly with each other without having to go through the formal hierarchical channels in order to get things done. This can be accomplished only by truly delegating the decision-making powers and equipping teams with self-governing privileges that transcend the remit of the line organization.

- Appoint only one boss per product. To avoid any procrastination that slows down the decision-making process, the project charter must appoint the single individual that holds sole power to recruit and dismiss team members, and, equally important, have the final say in approving or rejecting deliverables. Whereas most organizations operate on matrix structures, where employees report to more than one manager, decision-making in innovation should not follow this model or rely on a committee structure.

- An often forgotten aspect, and in hindsight appearing remarkably surprisingly so, is the lack of in-house recognition of innovations. The case of Kodak, which held a huge number of patents, is exemplary. However, most were not brought forward and recognized by senior management, being left unattended to and not being commercially exploited. This as Kodak clung on to its legacy products that were becoming more and more outdated, eventually causing its demise, forcing it into bankruptcy as it could no longer match technically more advanced competitors. Especially in large corporations, it is not unusual for new innovative products and services to be not inadequately socialized among the ranks, such as being promoted to the sales teams. This is attributable to lack of senior management commitment, or even an angst of what havoc they might create internally, as they hold the potential to render existing products with its affiliated organizational structure obsolete. Here the C-level sponsors must show true leadership, taking charge of the internal marketing and making the necessary organizational changes, however initially painful, to ensure profits can be optimized from the new innovative products and can be fully leveraged from existing, or as required adjusted, distribution channels.[16]

Formulating an Organizational Blueprint for Innovation

By applying the insights into how innovation happens, how it is best administered, and in what environment it may flourish, a high-level organizational blueprint can be formulated to provide aspiring market leaders, regardless of industry, with inspirational pointers. It should be contrasted with how the creative spirit perishes in a desolate overregulated setting. Recognizing that the chances of recruiting that one-of-a-kind lonely genius that (occasionally) comes up with transformational ideas are slim, corporations should instead seek to establish teams on the basis of collective intelligence with a focus on the less serendipitous types of innovation—exploratory and combinational. With the steps of the creative process identified and ascertained, they provide a sequence on how work on innovation can be structured, pinning out differing roles and responsibilities for each step throughout. Efforts are guided by a holistic leadership. The input parameters will help in forming the building blocks required to produce an abstract representation that constitutes the basis for generating scenarios in the incubation phase. The normal protocol for experimental testing typically includes only variations within the preset assumptions and context. But herein lies a conundrum: the process of creativity with a view to producing new innovative thinking differs from traditional problem-solving given its complexity. It typically lacks a solution that is known in advance, and the problem in itself is usually never exactly defined. Hence, if a solution cannot be found within these narrow parameters, the work risk comes to a standstill. It is in this phase and the ensuing illumination phase that the lonely genius types tend to prove their worth, generating value-adding scenarios that can occasionally materialize as a viable solution, often falling far outside the existing scientific or commercial doctrine, which makes it so hard for the average expert to replicate. Historical hindsight shows it is in that realm that scientific breakthroughs often occur. From the cognitive perspective, it is an iterative process that arranges the search by narrowing down the key determinants and a potentially correct path often acknowledged by an intuitive subjective feel-good factor, as highlighted by Poincaré. The next step is to start to home in on that particular path in search of a conclusion. So, in complex problem-solving, the incubation phase draws heavily on the seemingly irrational associations that are made in the unconscious part of the mind. This is done with a view to breaking the mental constraints that prevent creative thinking, which is typically limited by the capacity of human imagination and the level of subject matter expertise. In the absence of the lonely genius, a collective intelligence approach may take a multivariate perspective to increase the chances of finding a solution. This can be done by applying imagination to a set problem by distorting some of the objects and relationships as a means of purposely skewing the mental representation to reach a higher representation of reality. At the heart of amalgamating individual human intelligence into a collective intelligence effort lies the ability to produce a suite of conceptual changes, instead of being mentally blocked by a single narrative. The power of collective intelligence efforts therefore rests in the following:

I. in its scenario generating capacity, which exceeds that of what the typical average individual is capable of, and

II. the ability to create random scenarios, even those of a bizarre nature, superseding that of normal human imagination.

Techniques for how to conduct such a wider scenario generation are detailed in the next chapter.

The scenario testing triggers a feedback-and-verification loop, set to repeat itself until a successful solution is found (if at all) that keeps reverting

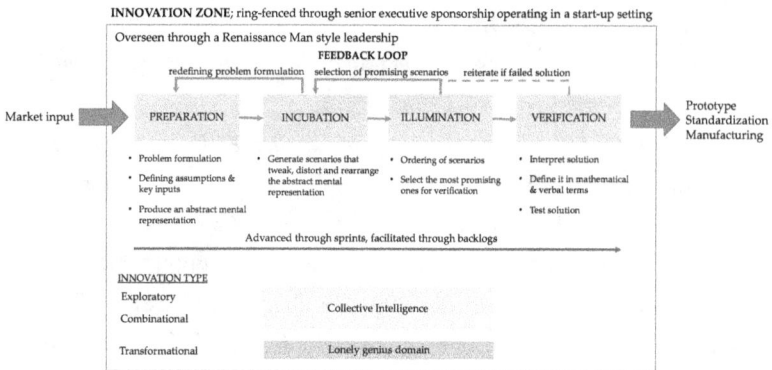

INNOVATION ZONE; ring-fenced through senior executive sponsorship operating in a start-up setting

Overseen through a Renaissance Man style leadership

FEEDBACK LOOP

redefining problem formulation   selection of promising scenarios   reiterate if failed solution

Market input → PREPARATION → INCUBATION → ILLUMINATION → VERIFICATION → Prototype Standardization Manufacturing

- Problem formulation
- Defining assumptions & key inputs
- Produce an abstract mental representation

- Generate scenarios that tweak, distort and rearrange the abstract mental representation

- Ordering of scenarios
- Select the most promising ones for verification

- Interpret solution
- Define it in mathematical & verbal terms
- Test solution

Advanced through sprints, facilitated through backlogs

INNOVATION TYPE

Exploratory

Combinational

Collective Intelligence

Transformational

Lonely genius domain

Figure 3.1 A graphic depiction highlighting the organizational blueprint for an innovative center of excellence

to the problem formulation and input data phase of the project with continuous calibration. Finally, the verification phase aims to formalize the solution, verbally, and as required mathematically, and commencing the test of the solution. Through the sprint format and backlog facilitation, the work is monitored for progress, and with a sign-off approving the test of the proposed solution, the development of a prototype, standardization and manufacturing will move the project into a new phase (Figure 3.1) .

Equipped with an understanding of how to most efficiently organize the workforce for innovation and how to promote creativity, a key question remains, namely, who is best suited to leading such an enterprise that often is both chaotic and complex?

Endnotes

1. T.S. Kuhn. 1996. *The Structure of Scientific Revolutions*. 3rd ed. (Chicago, IL: Chicago University Press).
2. G. Wallas. 2014. *The Art of Thought* (Kent, UK: Solis Press).
3. Ibid.
4. Ibid.
5. H. Poincaré. 1910. "Mathematical Creation," *The Monist* 20, no. 3, pp. 321-35.
6. K.J. Gilhooly. 2016. "Incubation and Intuition in Creative Problem Solving," *Frontiers in Psychology* 7, p. 1076.

7. U.N. Sio and T.C. Ormerod. January 2009. "Does Incubation Enhance Problem Solving? A Meta-analytic Review," *Psychological Bulletein* 135, no. 1, pp. 94-120.

8. R. Ochse. 1990. *Before the Gates of Excellence: The Determinants of Creative Genius* (New York, NY: Cambridge University Press).

9. M.A. Runco. 2006. *Creativity and Reason in Cognitive Development* (Cambridge, UK: Cambridge University Press), pp. 99-116.

10. R. Sternberg and T. Lubart. 1999. *The Concept of Creativity: Prospects and Paradigms. Handbook of Creativity* (London, UK: Cambridge University Press), Vol. 1, pp. 3-15.

11. L. Gabora. *Cognitive Mechanisms Underlying the Origin and Evolution of Culture* [Doctoral thesis]. Brussels, Belgium: Free University of Brussels, 2001.

12. R.J. Hollingsworth and E.J. Hollingsworth. 2011. *Major Discoveries, Creativity, and the Dynamics of Science (Complexity Design Society, 15)* (Vienna, Austria: Remaprint Wien).

13. G. Törnqvist. 2004. *Kreativitetens geografi* (Stockholm: SNS Förlag).

14. M.A. Boden. 2004. *The Creative Mind: Myths and Mechanisms* (London, UK: Routledge).

15. D.K. Rigby, J. Sutherland, and H. Takeuchi. May 2016. "Embracing Agile," *Harvard Business Review.* https://hbr.org/2016/05/embracing-agile (accessed 1 June 2020).

16. D.K. Rigby, S. Berez, G. Caimi, and A. Noble. 19 April 2016. "Agile Innovation," *Bain & Company, Insights.* https://www.bain.com/insights/agile-innovation/ (accessed 1 June 2020).

CHAPTER 4

The Renaissance Man

*Every age has a kind of universal genius, which inclines those that
live in it to some particular studies.*
—John Dryden, English poet (1631 to 1700)

The Historical Renaissance Man

The Renaissance Period, which stretched from the 14th through the 17th
centuries, originated in Italy and spread to the rest of Europe. It is probably best remembered for its many exceptionally gifted individuals, a
good deal of them of Italian extraction, and hence the term *renaissance
man*. To most people, Leonardo Da Vinci immediately comes to mind; he
was considered the renaissance man extraordinaire, being the archetype
of the universal genius. He had exceptional knowledge in a number of
disciplines; art, engineering, medicine, philosophy, science, technologies,
and the humanities. His brilliance was manifested through work that has
immortalized him and that everyone is familiar with. This includes paint-
ings like *Mona Lisa* and *The Last Supper*. In science and technology, he
conceptualized flying machines and constructed state-of-the-art bridges,
and in medicine he dissected corpses that gave him a unique understanding, at the time, of the human body. But there was far more to Da Vinci
than the vast knowledge he possessed and the exquisite way he displayed
it. Studying his life and exploits produces the definite impression of the
man being on a quest to better understand the world by examining it
from a multitude of perspectives. A somewhat boastful definition of what
it meant to be a renaissance man was coined by the Italian Leon Battista
Alberti (1404 to 1472), who himself certainly qualified for the title, as
an architect, painter, horseman, archer, and inventor: "a man can do all
things if he will."[1] If nothing else, this definition really highlights the

aspirations of the renaissance man, a person seeking to acquire a broad base of knowledge and meaningfully deploy it in intellectual, artistic, spiritual, and physical pursuits. The uniqueness of the renaissance era was that humans were regarded as limitless, and the ideal was to openly embrace knowledge and develop oneself to the extent possible. This objective was guided by the chivalresque ideals of the time, and how to conduct oneself properly was part and parcel of this ambition. But it required a change in the hitherto fragmented educational system, as a truly universal education was needed. So, universities were established, providing a coordinated educational focal point where a raft of subjects could be studied under the same roof. Although the physical arrangement has survived till current times, the curriculum has not. For the aspiring renaissance men, not only was there a need for a deep knowledge of various academic subjects, which were a designated mixture of arts, science, and humanities, in particular from the perspective of Christian doctrine, but there was also a strong emphasis on rhetorical skills and the ability to express oneself eloquently in writing, including poetry. To this came requirements of physical prowess, engaging in various types of sports, all filling some military purpose, such as archery and fencing. This was nicely packaged by at the same time grooming the students into becoming perfect gentlemen. The argument was that a broad base of knowledge would provide a holistic worldview by amalgamating different perspectives and models. From there on, the students could progress by specializing in one or several disciplines as desired. The gist of this pedagogy was to develop a capacity for lateral thinking. This was thought to enhance the level of subject matter expertise by applying analogies from one discipline to another, as these acted as cognitive bridges between different subjects and worked as enablers to solve complex problems. But a renaissance man was also expected to have certain personal characteristics to be able to grasp this comprehensive education, Leonardo Da Vinci being a case in point, a person described as having an unquenchable curiosity and a highly inventive imagination.[2] In all, the levels of knowledge were expected to reach *sprezzatura*, meaning, mastering a skill so well as to be able to perform it with ease, and also with a capacity to contribute positively to it.[3] Of course, but rarely explicitly stated at the time, not anyone could become a renaissance man, irrespective of money and pedigree. A minimum cognitive level was assumed in order to be able to simultaneously comprehend a number of intellectually demanding topics paired with a capacity for abstract thinking.

Modern Interpretations of the Renaissance Man

The term "renaissance man" is rarely used today, probably sounding too pompous. Instead, polymath is the preferred label, with a definition that is more elastic, removing the stringent requirements from the medieval times. It has come to mean a person with broad-based knowledge in many areas, and expertise in one or a couple of these, but does not specify how this body of knowledge should be composed. Thus, there is no requirement of mixing natural science, technology, humanities, and the arts. It also does not come with any particular obligations as to levels of articulation or presentation and literary skills. More concerning, perhaps, is that being a polymath is no longer an aspiring ideal for the average university student and has not really been for generations. However, some research efforts are being directed into the question of how best to educate polymaths in the current academic setting, although few of these insights have been practically implemented. American academic Robert Root-Bernstein, who has focused some of his research on creativity, the universality of the creative process, in particular, has used these insights as a basis upon which to develop a polymath curriculum.[4,5] Root-Bernstein argues that rather than creativity being a domain-specific phenomenon, such as bespoke for poets vis-à-vis physicists, there are certain creative features that can be applied independent of expertise domain. He views the polymath as being particularly suited to integrating concepts across disciplines. It is, in particular, the free-flowing meaningful blending between domains that can produce creative value-adding ideas. He contends that polymaths are therefore expected to be at the forefront of innovation and that the educational system should be designed to nurture them with a particular focus to strengthen their creative ability.[6] Root-Bernstein details the definition of polymaths through six types;

- Type 1, the prodigy that right from an early age excels in a particular area, through talent and hard work, even to the point of being obsessive, and keeps at it all through life; Wolfgang Amadeus Mozart being an example;

- Type 2, the intellectually curious who dabbles in a number of intellectual areas and eventually settles for one of these;
- Type 3, the type most resembling the original renaissance man, individuals that from outset acquire in-depth knowledge, even expertise, in several areas, and stays engaged in them throughout life;
- Type 4, also a prodigy type but that, over time, also explores other intellectual areas and develops excellence in these as well;
- Type 5, the serial polymath that keeps exploring one creative field after another through a voracious curiosity throughout life; and
- Type 6, a sort of mixture between type 3 and type 5.[7]

Hence, today, a renaissance man might come in a variety of forms, but why does it seem that there are so much fewer of them now than before? Well, one explanation is that generalist careers are not encouraged in the business world and that therefore individuals with the capability to become renaissance men refrain from doing so as there is no financial pay-off to it. An engineering-like approach still dominates digital transformations, mainly because it provides a sense of precision that gives a comfortable feeling of exactness. Therefore, technical specialists are almost exclusively recruited to lead them. But as anyone who has been through a few digital transformations knows, estimates made at the onset of projects will deviate considerably from the end-results; yet this false sense of security is deeply rooted. Any perspectives deviating from the engineering mindset are viewed suspiciously, as they cannot provide this precision, albeit false. Also, generalists are often looked down upon by the specialists as they lack the depth of knowledge in that particular domain and are hence seen as less knowledgeable. But because their perspective is so overwhelmingly singular (read: tech), they miss impacts from other areas that often derail the intended results of digital transformations.

However, there are also practical reasons. British historian Peter Burke presents the widely held view that the decline of the renaissance man coincided with the rapid advancement of science from the 17th century onwards, making it increasingly harder to be concurrently on top of a variety of intellectual topics. Specialization therefore became necessary, as time and energy limited the possibilities to keep up to date and master a raft of academic disciplines. According to him, a regression was bound to occur *"from knowledge in every [academic] field to knowledge in several fields, and from making original contributions in many fields to a more passive consumption of what has been contributed by others."*[8,9]

To Burke, the proactive manner in which the renaissance man of medieval times was expected to carry himself has, owing to the increased workload required, instead turned him into a passive polymath. He is still adept at acquiring huge amounts of knowledge on a plethora of topics, and at times is also a decent amateur athlete and/or artist, but is nowadays rarely capable of contributing productively to a domain other than the one in which he has specialized in. Burke argues that in our age of specialization, which has further narrowed down since the 17th century, with ever more distinct academic disciplines, the world actually needs polymaths more than ever. The ability is needed to transcend and see the bigger picture, rather than being domain myopic, with a capability to synthesize models and concepts from different scientific narratives to gain a more thorough understanding of reality:

> *It takes a polymath to "mind the gap" and draw attention to the knowledges that may otherwise disappear into the spaces between disciplines, as they are currently defined and organized.*[10]

But how were the renaissance men of yesteryear as well as the polymaths of today able to generate these innovative value-adding ideas that have advanced science in such dramatic ways? A body of studies have researched creative thinking, which highlights a number of shared patterns, all with the common denominator of thinking outside the proverbial box, in essence, seeking a multitude of perspectives and being equipped with the capacity to formulate these insights accordingly. It provides templates of how this lateral type thinking, in theory at least, can be applied, all bearing the hallmarks of renaissance man style conceptualization. Some of the key ones among these are;

- Looking at problems from many perspectives, with many paradigm shift-type innovations seeing their advent through ideas considered unconventional because they were violating the reigning (scientific) narrative. Restructuring a problem in many variations by applying different models is a constructive method to draw out possible solutions but also an exercise of looking at a problem from different angles, which in itself will deepen the understanding of the problem. Another approach is to specifically seek out the details that do not fit in in accordance with the existing explanatory models, as a mean of exploring whether these can give rise to alternative insights that help reconceptualize the problem.

• Articulate ideas and possible solutions through written composition and illustrations. The education of the renaissance man ensured that they were well versed both as painters and as poets and possessed a rich vocabulary and an ability to graphically represent abstractions, and physical objects—an exercise that was seen as enhancing their capacity to adequately formulate problems and their solutions. Later on, Albert Einstein testified to his visual and spatial abilities when working on a problem, often depicting it in various images, emphasizing its advantages over just mathematically and verbally expressing it.

• Although poetry might not be the preferred form of articulating innovative ideas today, polymaths do tend to allow metaphors and symbolic language to represent their thoughts, such as seeking out resemblances between two separate, rarely interlinked, areas, in particular making novel combinations and using known features to describe the unknown.

• The juxtaposition of diverging subjects as a method to create captivating and intellectually valuable phenomena was a staple for the renaissance man, sometimes deliberately mixing and matching opposites, by identifying a common denominator, however miniscule. It allowed for connecting the seemingly unconnected, and for an amalgamation to form, that occasionally produced something value-added that changed perspective, advancing art and science.

• The highly demanding curriculum the renaissance men went through fostered a work ethic that, until today, has remained unmatched, something that remained with many of them having an immense productivity across domains throughout their lives.[11–15]

The medieval requirements of becoming a renaissance man, when translated into today's perspective, would include having in-depth knowledge in several academic disciplines, including expertise status in at least one, or more likely a couple of them, spanning across art, natural sciences, social sciences, and technology. They would be able to, in elegant prose, write research papers that advanced their chosen subjects, present them with oratory poise, to that excel in both the arts and athletics, and at all times conduct themselves in a courteous and honorable manner. Indeed a tall order, and the renaissance man ideal has long been dropped as a role model for tertiary institutions, seeming too arcane, possibly too elitist, and, above all, with the increasing degree of specialization in both academia and the commercial world, there appears to be a lack of demand for individuals that are truly masters of all trades.

The benefits of having a wide range of knowledge have also been noted in forecasting, where people who are good at a multitude of domains make more accurate predictions about the future than specialists in the particular domain. This insight was highlighted in the *Good Judgment Project*, an initiative funded by the U.S. government's Intelligence Advanced Research Project, which sought methods on trying to improve geopolitical forecasting. The study highlights that it is not the knowledge itself but rather a capacity for active, open-minded thinking and applying a scientific deductive approach to look rigorously at available data that improves accuracy in forecasts. Specialist knowledge appears at times to impose a given narrative on situations that make interpretations inflexible as they come too much to rest on certain assumptions. These super forecasters, as they were referred to, were much more willing to consider unorthodox ideas or results and not get overly attached to one particular viewpoint, unlike a specialist, who often forced new information into a preexisting mental framework or discarded it if it seemed to contradict their initial view.[16]

One of the key questions then becomes, *can anyone become a renaissance man?* Is it merely a question of reading up on the raft of topics that are relevant for digital transformations? In short, no, because there are also requirements of a personal nature, something already recognized in medieval times, including;

- a cognitive capacity to be able to fathom highly abstract theories;
- an intellectual curiosity with a thirst for knowledge and new experiences;

- being a risk taker rather than risk averse, with a distinct entrepreneurial flair;
- having creative capabilities;
- having perseverance and the resilience to see things through; and
- the leadership skills stemming from both cognitive authority and superior people management, allowing for both coaching and, when necessary, crisis management "command and control."

Basically, it is a person defined by having both high IQ and EQ and driven by an enormous curiosity. The renaissance man is fascinated by existing and emerging technical possibilities and an acumen and eagerness to make productive sense of these in a diffuse and fast-changing environment. There is a constant desire to find value-added solutions to commercial opportunities and problems. It is a combination of "the thinking man" and "the action man" that manages people through a can-do spirit and can act as a high-energy coach and crisis leader interchangeably.

Why the Renaissance Man Is Ideal to Lead in the Digital Age

As businesses embark on digital transformations, it often becomes apparent to them that the traditional management styles are not adequate. They render results far below initial expectations, providing half-baked digital solutions where potential commercial gains are poorly captured and leveraged, or simply not even identified. Mismatches between technologies, the man–machine (dis-)connect, or organizational dysfunctionality are typically identified as root causes, but beneath them lurks a more scathing problem: an inadequate leadership. And it is generally not because of a lack of technological expertise or poor people management; these skills are often sufficiently resourced. The leadership problem is instead of a more imperative nature, particularly as the digital transformation comes to challenge the business to its core; how do we provide customer value? How do we organize us in the most (cost-)efficient way? In effect, it strikes at the heart of a corporation's raison d'être and, as such, goes far beyond technical solutions, organizational structure, or indeed even an in-depth understanding of products and markets. A digital transformation, explicitly (and implicitly) transcends all of these perspectives in its aspiration toward value maximation. By acknowledging these cojoined complexities, the elements on what it is that the digital leadership requires can be formulated, namely, a holistic approach capable of incorporating them, facilitated by a cognitive capacity able to craft commercially viable products and services. However, individuals with such diverse skills and experiences are rarely sought after, because corporations in our age of the specialists that are drilling down in ever more granular minutiae tend to regard generalists somewhat suspiciously. They will insist on appointing seasoned technical specialists leading the implementation of digital tools instead. But if one accepts the proposition that digital transformations mean much more than installing a piece of software, and although the technical aspects of such projects are important as they must also be understood and viewed in a much broader context, a generalist perspective becomes mission critical. The generalist leaders are capable of, through a kaleidoscope of perspectives, evaluate the business model, the organization and its employees as well as the markets it operates in, in the selection of digital strategies. This holistic perspective also applies to tactical executions thereof. However, if the leadership is equipped only with technical skills, the focus on the transformation will be far too myopic, and the additional consideration will be neglected because they are not fully understood or capitalized on. Instead, the digital transformation becomes nothing but an uncoordinated fragmented *smörgåsbord* approach, inevitably spending considerably more time and more money than what is justified. It also has a psychological cost, in that it loses important momentum because individual projects are not harmonized into a unified strategy, eventually creating the risk of project fatigue among the employees. From this viewpoint, the renaissance man leadership model appears alluring, although applying a medieval role model to the digital world is sure to be considered by some as anachronistic. However, if thoroughly considered, it might not be as far-fetched as it first sounds. Its value lies in the deliberate blend of skills, which span a wide variety of areas, albeit modified to suit the knowledge requirements necessary to lead digital transformations. Such a knowledge base enables a holistic perspective to truly fathom an all-encompassing corporate revitalization. Obviously, the expectation is not to seek out or to groom the Leonardo Da Vinci or Michelangelo of today but rather to educate already recognized good leadership material, typically with a background in technology, in a bespokenly chosen raft of subjects, arranged to improve their ability to successfully lead digital transformations. Although arts and alchemy, certainly in themselves enviable endeavors and mandatory for yesteryear's renaissance men, might not be part of the curriculum to develop the ideal digital leader of today, aesthetics still plays a vital role. In the current setting, that would mean an understanding of the craftsmanship required to design and develop products and services, and the design thinking principles that such efforts rest on. The ambition for the digital renaissance man remains which is the ability to view and comprehend, through deliberately acquired skills, a highly mosaic commercial world from its many facets. The renaissance men provided an insight that has stood the test of time, namely, that an all-embracing generalist can surpass the singular specialist in solving complex real-world problems by dissecting and inspecting them from a variety of perspectives. They did so by applying analogies and different models across disciplines, as they uniquely managed to tie together distinctive disciplines' concepts and jargon. Thus, beyond the obvious qualifications of being a leader of people and possessing a profound understanding of digital technologies, preferably bolstered through a solid foundation of psychology and mathematics, respectively, to all this comes an in-depth acumen of the markets with its existing offerings of products and services. It also incorporates a knowledge of the legal frameworks surrounding it as well as the various trends and fads (whether of a cultural, economic, or political nature) that influence customer preferences now and in the future. An equally important skill is the ability to eloquently articulate the methodologies and models that allow for an improved understanding of what the digital economy really means. A literary ability is pivotal to succinctly and precisely formulate and convey strategies. Sadly, it is a skill all but lost among today's executives that have been too marinated in monosyllabic PowerPoint consultant speak and platitudes. Hence, they are only occasionally capable of coherently articulating a full paragraph, let alone a comprehensive report. Being versatile in all of the aforementioned key areas, the digital renaissance man is ideally positioned to successfully lead agile cross-functional teams, able to fully fathom each and every specialist's point of view, and being fluent in *Agilian*, able to integrate and augment these into an all-encompassing implementation that better reflects realities.

But Do Not Expect the Educational System to Embrace the Renaissance Man Ethos Anytime Soon

The current educational system is developed on a doctrine that promotes the specialist, with individual academic disciplines jealously guarding their sources of funding and intellectual domains against any infringements from "competing" faculties. If anything, specialization has, over time, advanced and morphed into a stream of cloning new disciplines with their distinct thought narratives and jargon, eagerly seeking to ring-fence themselves through singular perspectives. This has rendered any academic cross-discipline ventures appearing only rarely. It is hardly fertile ground for anyone seeking a generalist's cultivation, and they will certainly not find it in the formerly much celebrated MBA degree. Once upon a time, it was praised by the corporate leaders of the 1980s as the management education supreme and was for a while all but mandatory for executives. Eventually, its perceived importance became grossly inflated, and it has not quite stood the test of time given the changing conditions on the ground, commencing with the *dot.com boom* of the 1990s. It is now largely considered obsolete as it remains entrenched in the outmoded case study pedagogy. So, sadly, the aspiring renaissance man will find that the tertiary education does not provide a diverse enough concoction of academic flavors accompanied by the associated training in lateral thinking and leadership. Hence, they are left to their own devices, and therefore often opt for the autodidact route trying to craft their own take of a versatile education.

There Is More Bad News; Your HR Department Is Going to Reject Applications from Renaissance Men

The intellectual curiosity and dynamism that form the renaissance men's personalities will be reflected in their résumés, typically featured through a peculiarly wide variation of both academic and work experiences. But that is not a résumé that will entice the HR department, who remain deeply rooted in seeking out candidates through a check-the-box approach, sometimes automated in its search for key words that are assumed to equate the desired skill sets. Any greater deviations from their standards will therefore be considered as rejects by default.

Human Resources' take on establishing diverse workplaces, although in itself a laudable aspiration, rests, however, on a flawed assumption, namely, that individuals can represent only one perspective at a time—possibly, a presumption that has its roots in identity politics. As a consequence, HR policies seek to devise the appropriate mix of employees by proactively recruiting stereotypes that are assumed to represent particular perspectives. These are not only defined by academic and professional qualifications but have been extended to various demographic components, where at times mathematical precision is sought to achieve the ideal workplace. It is then assumed that a multitude of perspectives will somehow manifest and enrich the workplace, ultimately translating into increased profits. The evidence of this actually occurring are far from conclusive, because candidates are not screened for a blend of idiosyncratic thought patterns but instead through assumed proxy attributes. Thus, the renaissance man, often being an autodidact with a highly diverse intellectual and cultural background, can hardly be boxed in to represent one particular perspective. So, when gauged through the simpleton tests which HR departments are arranging its candidate scans by, is sure to be eliminated, often already at the initial stage of the recruitment process. This represents a great loss to the business that will miss out on a future employee equipped with a wide knowledge diversity, ideally suited to leading, rather than managing, digital transformations.

Endnotes

1. Encyclopaedia Britannica. "Renaissance man." https://www.britannica.com/topic/Renaissance-man (accessed 1 June 2020).
2. H. Gardner. 1970. *Art through the Ages*. 5th ed. (New York, NY: Harcourt, Brace & World), pp. 450-6.
3. B. Castiglione. 2002. *The Book of the Courtier* (translated by Charles S. Singleton, New York, NY: W.W. Norton) (original *Il Cortegiano*, Aldine Press, 1528), pp. 319-28.

4. R. Root-Bernstein. 2003. "The Art of Innovation: Polymaths and Universality of the Creative Process." In *The International Handbook on Innovation*, ed. L.V. Shavinina. Amsterdam: Elsevier, pp. 267-78.

5. L. Shavinina. 2013. "How to Develop Innovators? Innovation Education for the Gifted," *Gifted Education International*, 29, no. 1, pp. 54-68.

6. R. Root-Bernstein and M.M. Root-Bernstein. 2011. "Life Stages of Creativity." In *Encyclopedia of Creativity, Reference Work*, ed. M.A. Runco and S.R. Pritzker. 2nd ed. Oxford: Elsevier, pp. 47-55.

7. R. Root-Bernstein and M.M. Root-Bernstein. 2017. "People, Passions, Problems: The Role of Creative Exemplars in Teaching for Creativity." In *Creative Contradictions in Education, Cross Disciplinary Paradoxes and Perspectives*, ed. R.A. Beghetto and B. Sriraman. Berlin: SpringerLink, pp. 143-64.

8. P. Burke. 2012. *A Social History of Knowledge II: From the Encyclopaedia to Wikipedia*. 1st ed. (Cambridge: Polity Press), Vol. 2.

9. P. Burke. 2010. "The Polymath: A Cultural and Social History of an Intellectual Species." In *Explorations in Cultural History: Essays for Peter McCaffery*, ed. D.F. Smith and H. Philsooph. Aberdeen: Centre for Cultural History, University of Aberdeen, pp. 67-79.

10. P. Burke. 2012. *A Social History of Knowledge II: From the Encyclopaedia to Wikipedia*. 1st ed. (Cambridge: Polity), Vol. 2, p. 183.

11. A. Rothenberg, C.R. Hausman, and N. Durham. 1976. *The Creativity Question* (Durham, UK: Duke University Press Books).

12. R.S. Albert and M.A. Runco. 1999. "A History of Research on Creativity." In *Handbook of Creativity*, ed. R.J. Sternberg. Cambridge: Cambridge University Press.

13. R. Ochse. 1990. *Before the Gates of Excellence: The Determinants of Creative Genius* (New York, NY: Cambridge University Press).

14. M.A. Runco. 2006. *Creativity and Reason in Cognitive Development* (Cambridge: Cambridge University Press).

15. R. Sternberg and T. Lubart. 1999. *The Concept of Creativity: Prospects and Paradigms. Handbook of Creativity* (London, UK: Cambridge University Press), Vol. 1.

16. P.E. Tetlock and D. Gardne. 2015. *Superforecasting: The Art and Science of Prediction*. 1st ed. (New York, NY: Crown).

CHAPTER 5

A Beautiful New World?

L'utopie est ce qui est en contradiction avec la réalité
(Utopia is that which is in contradiction with reality)
—Albert Camus,
French philosopher (1913 to 1960)

Few are unaware of the drastic changes that the ongoing digital transformation initiatives have wrought on the commercial world. But when all industries, in various degrees, have been digitalized, will that cumulatively also affect our societies? If so, how? Are we experiencing what in effect is a bottom-up revolution driven by this technological paradigm shift?

We already know that the digital economy is quite specific and demanding in terms of the kind of employees it is looking for, so what will that do to the educational system? Can it affect our welfare programs, and what about demographics? History shows that drastic economic changes come with *Malthusian* effects on birth rates. Is this the case now as well? And can this all-encompassing digital transformation also extend to politics? Are we set for an unavoidable conflict between top-down authoritarian governing models versus the digital economy, which, by design, seeks to break down hierarchies to promote innovation and individualism?

Does the Digital Economy Equal the Digital Society?

Beginning well before the millennia shift, a number of long-term ongoing structural changes have been affecting our economies and, by extension, our societies. These changes have sprung from multiple sources: the deindustrialization of OECD countries, partly owing to outsourcing of employment to low-cost countries, but also increased automation, which is now starting to impact the higher-end service sectors. This has resulted in a declining labor participation rate, creating an overextended welfare state that in most countries can be maintained only through increased lending. It is leading to such excessive debt burdens that countries, municipalities, and individuals are, in various degrees, heading toward bankruptcy. But life is not gloomy for everyone; an exclusive group of people whose skill sets are highly sought after in the fast growing knowledge-based sectors of the economy have noted little, if anything, of these destructive developments. We are seeing the emergence of an economic system with binary characteristics, broadly split between the ones that qualify for the digital economy and the ones that are not. It is, unfortunately, a model that only marginally allows for transitory shifts between these two segments, and what makes matters worse is that most of these shifts will be downward. If being considered value-adding you will be part of the digital nobility, a salutation that, like its original meaning, can actually come to prove hereditary. Making a fortune in a record time, by legal means at least, has never been as easy—just ask the mundane tech start-up gazillionaire. But if you do not qualify as a contributing digital worker or entrepreneur, your future might actually never begin. Hence, the notion of an evolving binary economy is apt, with a prosperous upper class enjoying the spoils of the knowledge-based economy and increasingly isolating themselves from society, and an exceedingly large *lumpen proletariat,* which for various reasons is unable to upgrade to the jobs that the digital economy has to offer. The traditional middle class in between is basically now reallocating in either direction, depending much more on their cognitive abilities than connections and pedigree. This new world is reflected in the deteriorating trends of many socioeconomic indicators that, until recently, only saw improvements, including educational standards, crime rates, and health levels, both physical and psychological. Many points to that the increasing psychological despair is due to a lack of hope, the upward path towards social mobility appears to have been cut off with little opportunity for the destitute to improve their situations. The *American Dream* and other rags-to-riches fairy tales are for many now just a pipe dream. Given the demanding cognitive capabilities, which has proven to be largely innate in character, that the well-paying jobs offered in the digital economy require, the prospects of broader advancements from an underclass perspective appears rather limited. Learning how to be a software developer *et al.* is truly challenging, and not many are up for it. What is more, the eventual payoffs for university exams seem to be diminishing as students, particularly in fields outside technology and natural sciences, struggle to find work, with slim prospects of paying off the record levels of accumulated student loans. The cementing and bifurcation of the economy come with highly detrimental social effects and a fear that these will extend into periods of social unrest, even spilling over into organized riots and violence with revolutionary tendencies.

And for many individual countries, it has come to mean a diminishing role because it can no longer afford to provide the previous full-scale services, given that increasing numbers of its citizens are in need of welfare and various entitlements are adding to a shrinking tax base. Many previously industrialized countries are both now and for the foreseeable future faced with a large underclass, which could extend to up to 50 percent of the entire population. These are unable to support themselves in the long term by being on the dole, perhaps permanently on welfare, or in and out of low-paying jobs that not will make ends meet. They have few opportunities to accumulate any savings or to allow for any greater capital investments to secure a livable pension income. The cost of supporting this underclass is now consuming so much of the tax revenues that it is eating into other commitments of the state, including education, healthcare, infrastructure, defense, and upholding of the law. For the state at large, these people will, over their lifetime, be a net cost, because their meager taxable incomes, if any, will by no means match their entitlements, and, what is more, they are hopelessly stuck with them. Addressing high unemployment through large-scale waves of emigration, of the kind that took place a century ago from Europe to North America, is no longer feasible; there is simply nowhere to go, no new frontiers to explore and exploit.

The Main Asset of the Digital Economy Is Cognitive Capital

Cognitive capital has become one of the key inputs in the digital economy. Immaterial assets created using the human mind as the only raw material have come to play an ever greater role in arranging and creating

economic growth. Human cognitive capital holds interesting characteristics not to be found in other assets, such as the absence of diminishing
returns. Essentially, one cannot have too much of it, and the potential
returns can be multiples of what any other asset can generate. Cognitive
capital can be defined as follows:

> ...cognitive ability predicts the quality of economic and political
> institutions, which further determines the economic affluence of
> the nation. Cognitive resources enable the evolution of capitalism
> and the rise of wealth.[1]

Obviously, the importance of education is not lost on any government as a means of enhancing its nation's cognitive capital, although it
is rarely articulated in those terms. But is it paying off? This is a question
that is potentially a political minefield, because it has been an unquestionable axiom that education is always going to be a worthwhile (social)
investment. It has in itself become a gigantic industry with students aspiring for a bright future. But many have been running up debts for tuition
fees that for some are now well beyond repayable levels unless their exams
can help them find high-paying positions. Cognitive capital is considered
essential to secure economic growth, on the basis of the traditional view
that it is as simple as throwing money at education and that each dollar
spent will over time provide a positive return on investment. To calcu-
late at the societal level the exact profit is more art than science, as the
payoff typically arrives after a considerable time lag, sometimes decades
later, and often indirectly, such as through increased income taxes. But as
important as education is, no conclusive evidence points to an intrinsic
obvious relationship between the size of investments in education and
economic growth. The ingredients for knowledge-based economies appear more elusive than just the level of formal education and the length
of it. Thus, measuring the factors influencing cognitive capital versus
GDP per capita growth is less obvious.[2,3] Evidence that cognitive capital,
rather than formal education, matters economically has been provided by
a research group, led by German psychologist Heiner Rindermann. They
applied IQ levels as a proxy measure for cognitive capital, which in itself
comes with considerable measurement problems. However, they found

a notable correlation, which they argued demonstrated the importance of the population's cognitive abilities, and, in particular, the so-called *smart fraction,* the top 5 percent of the IQ ranking. Through a review of 90 countries and their respective estimated IQ levels and GDP per capita, Rindermann *et.al.* showed that for each point by which the average IQ improves, the GDP per capita increases by 229 US dollars. The difference became even larger if the smart fraction improved their IQ on average by one point, with the increase in GDP per capita being 468 US dollars.[4] As part of their research, they highlighted that cognitive ability is more important for economic development than the degree of economic freedom. Thus, countries with significant state interventions can still prove to be more economically successful as long as their populations have a higher IQ level, especially for the smart fraction, than a completely open and liberal free market economy.[5] 108 has been estimated as the IQ threshold for the smart fraction, and the proportion of a population above that threshold best predicts GDP per capita; obviously, the more of them a country has, the better for the economy, *ceteris paribus.*[6] This smart fraction group is imperative not only for the economy, but also for progress in all types of academia, culture, and innovation. The importance of this group has also been recognized in other studies, sometimes labeled *the creative class,* albeit not defined in terms of IQ levels but through various attributes such as the type of works they hold and the cultural activities they tend to engage in.[7]

Hence, increasing the smart fraction of the population is what seems to provide the best financial returns. But cognitive capacity, proxy measured through IQ, has been proved by numerous studies to be stubbornly stable. In short, it means that the hereditary influence is strong and, surprisingly enough, increases with age. One of the best examples of IQ stability was the famous *Lothian birth-cohort studies of 1921 and 1936,* covering almost all children born in Scotland in the respective years. It sought to study how IQ scores in childhood related to IQ scores in adolescence, extending to the advancing years. The Lothian studies are the longest continued studies of intelligence from childhood to old age and are still ongoing. The conclusion is that the IQ level in childhood does not deviate much from the IQ level that the individual will have throughout adulthood. In other words, education cannot do much to increase it. The studied birth cohorts ranged across all socioeconomic groups. The cohorts began their lives in a Scotland that was then an agricultural or early industrial society, regardless of the social class they belonged to, saw huge improvements in their environment over the decades. Healthcare advanced enormously, and access to education and information were greatly facilitated. To many participants, it was essentially an upgrade from a Third World country to a First World society. Yet despite these huge environmental improvements, the IQ levels over time changed little, individually as well as collectively. It has yet to be noted that a single individual has been able to increase his IQ from an average, or even relatively high, score to something akin to genius level. It is not so much a question of nature or nurture but rather what nurture that nature will enable.[8,9]

To make matters worse for most countries, the group of unem- ployables in the digital economy is bound to increase at an accelerating rate, mainly as automation, artificial intelligence, and robots continue to replace manufacturing and service work and are now also affecting higher-end types of work, including accounting, finance, and law. It is perhaps most notable in financial services, which for long were remark- ably reliant on increasing staff numbers and physical presence for growth. This is less so now. For many who possess specialized knowledge in ac- counting, finance, and law but lack the skills required for the brave new world of the man–machine—really, mostly machine—connect (read: IT skills), that dreaded phone call from HR is always lurking around the corner. This rationalization of labor moves forward more swiftly than the first wave of automation during the period of industrialization, which started in the mid-19th century and progressed over the next century. Some of the projections are dire indeed, and large parts of the labor force have been likened to the way the demand for workhorses plummeted in the early 20th century, never to return. Adding to the problem is that the leading global high-tech giants do not require a great number of employ- ees to hold monopoly or oligopoly positions worldwide. Facebook has about 43,000 employees, Google about 119,000, Apple 137,000, and Microsoft 151,000, each of them with a global reach. A university degree, especially in the social sciences, no longer guarantees employment; there is a documented decline in the demand for workers with tertiary educa- tion, whereas their supply has increased. Thus, the barista with a master's degree in gender studies or the likes working at Starbucks has come to serve as a figurehead for this phenomenon, where high-skilled, basically over-overeducated workers, are crowding out the less cognitively skilled ones as they move into low-skilled, low-paid positions.[10] There have long been hopes that somehow a new wave of work would be created en masse, in industries not easily operated by bots or robots, such as tourism and recreation, which would pick up the slack. However, until now, these aspirations have failed to materialize.

The selection criteria to join the digital economy appear brutal, but can one speak of discrimination? Certainly, though not through the common clusters of race or gender but through IQ discrimination. A high-tech firm cannot be forced to hire employees with an IQ level that goes below productive capability; it would severely hamper its chances of prospering and surviving in markets that already at the best of times are characterized by cut-throat competition. Although it is certainly true that other qualities are needed as well, including grit, productivity, and tenacity, a minimum level of IQ remains the starting point for even being considered.

Did Malthus Actually Foresee the Impact Digital Transformations Would Have on Birth Rates?

The gist of English cleric Thomas Malthus' (1766 to 1834) theories was that if a population grew too large, it would activate what he referred to as "positive checks," such as epidemics, wars, famines, and disasters, which would then reduce the population level to more sustainable numbers. But, more interestingly, Malthus also saw that mankind itself could proactively adjust the population levels through various demographic controls, but that these were often conducted in an unspoken implicit manner, and suddenly birth rates would just start to drop. It appeared that there existed some internal control mechanism that regulated birth rates, also in precontraception times, adjusting them to a more viable economic future.[11]

His hypothesis has been shown to forecast birth rates remarkably well as they coincide with the peaks and troughs of the economy, and the fact that recessions lead to falling birth rates has been noted historically.

During the Great Depression of the 1930s, the average size of a family dropped from three to two children. But there are also structural factors to consider: With the exception of the World War II-related baby boom years in the 1940s, the number of births per woman has continued to drop, regardless of economic cycles, and are below replacement level, not only in the United States but also in most of the other OECD countries. As women increasingly began entering academia and the work force from the 1950s onward, and as contraceptives and abortions became readily available, all these factors created a dampening effect, bringing about lasting alterations in fertility patterns.[12,13]

But a peculiar demographic phenomenon occurred after the financial crisis of 2008. At first, as expected, in the years after the crisis the birth rates fell, but as the economies started to recover, the birth rates still continued to fall. This has puzzled many demographers, and what is even more intriguing is that groups with historically higher numbers of child births, notably the lower socioeconomic groups, have, for the first time, seen their birth rates fall below the replacement rate of 2.1 children, something that is happening in most OECD countries. In contrast, well-to-do families now have more children than ever. It appears that having children, and a lot of them at that, has become the prerogative of the rich.

Why is this? It is because the recovering economy has failed to lift the overall labor force participation rate; on the contrary, it has continued to fall in many countries. Potential workers have either stopped looking for work altogether and are hence not part of the unemployment statistics (possibly partaking in the black economy) or are still studying, extending their studies with extra courses because they cannot find the desired employment. Whatever be the reason, the consequence has a dire effect on birth rates, as fewer and fewer youngsters appear not to be in a financial position to start a family. It could be that the post-2008 financial recovery has not succeeded in creating "real" job opportunities but rather work of an interim nature with poor economic prospects, and also that disintegrating welfare systems are taking their toll on planned pregnancies. If so, the blame has to be put on continued automation and digital transformation initiatives by corporates that have eliminated plenty of so-called low skill work but also a lot of entry-level positions for students. The ones that remain are mostly of a temporary nature with few long-term career prospects. This has had a direct impact on the economic situation of low educated groups, in particular, and subsequently their formation of families. In 2018, the birth rate among women of fertile age in the United States reached a record low of 59.0 births per 1,000 women (15 to 44 years old), despite an overall improving economy. The total fertility rate was 1.73 births per 1,000 women, the lowest since 1984, and well below the replacement rate. The numbers of unplanned pregnancies, which are typically concentrated among young girls in the lowest socioeconomic groups, have come down significantly. The birth rate for teenage girls has dropped dramatically over the last two decades to 20.3 births per 1,000 women between 15 and 19 years old in 2018, 67 percent lower than its last peak in 1991. Similar tendencies can be noted in most other OECD countries. Historically, as the economy improved, fertile women tended to play catch-up in later years, but this is not occurring now. The reproductive window for the millennial generation is now closing fast, and it is likely that many of these women struggling with financial security might forgo children altogether—a decision reinforced by facilitated access to contraceptives and abortion clinics, which, regardless of the peaks and troughs of the economy, reduced the birth rates further. Putting it more dramatically, it has become a sort of suicide of one's bloodline by deciding to perpetually terminate the genetic lineage from the human DNA pool. So this time it really appears to be different. Even though economic growth resumed a few years ago, falling birth rates still prevail among many categories that traditionally show high nativity: the unemployed, the underemployed, the undereducated, teenagers, minorities, and second-generation immigrants. Almost all of these groups have now fallen below replacement level and will see a shrinking population over the next generation, shifting the demographic distribution.[14–18]

You Cannot Have Both: Farewell Authoritarianism and Welcome Dissent

The digital economy, embraced through the agile mindset, is designed to confront existing business practices in a quest not only to do things better and faster but also to provide the customer with individualized commercial experiences. It implicitly seeks to eliminate bureaucracies and hierarchies by streamlining through digital means. To challenge everything is an essential part of this way of thinking. Being proactive, taking initiatives, and trying to see the world through different perspectives than what existing norms prescribe capture the very core of this digital philosophy. It would be naïve to believe that this mindset stops outside the business world. Once unleashed, and encouraged as a normative form of thinking, it is going to question all types of preconceived 'this is the way we have always done things' practices.

On the other hand, authoritarian political systems, of which there are far too many, rest on their citizens' adherence not to question certain dogmatic fundaments, notably their claim to power. These are imposed through early indoctrination and through a management-by-fear approach. Implicitly, every authoritarian leader, politician, or corporate executive wants its subjects to function as part of a big machinery, highly predictable, never obstinate or rebellious, and with any changes to the system only instigated in a top-down fashion. If there is one thing that dictators hate, it is instability, in whatever shape or form, because they know that it might come to threaten their reign in one way or another. They go to great lengths to eliminate it at all costs, or at least censor the acknowledgment of its existence. But as noted in a previous chapter, structural instability has proven to be something of a prerequisite for innovations. It provides that chaotic setting that all through history has acted as a highly fertile ground for creativity, where doctrines and dogma are torn apart and reassembled and where for a moment everything is allowed to be questioned. Iconic Spanish painter Pablo Picasso was once quoted as saying that "*every act of creation is first of all an act of destruction.*" At first glance, Picasso's comment might completely contradict the very definition of creativity, but the act of creating something innovative is often preceded by challenging and confronting preconceived notions and assumptions governing how to do things. In its most transformational quintessence, creativity is an attack on the normative thought patterns that stand as the doctrine of a particular scientific edifice or even a society and its political ideology. In the words of Thomas Kuhn, a creative breakthrough can signify a paradigm shift. The problem dictators have with creativity is that it transcends all areas of human activity, not only science but also arts and politics, and it can become contagious and set trends that reverberate throughout society. A noted psychological truth, while rarely recognized in an authoritarian setting, is that creativity brings with it a dynamism that is basically uncontrollable and comes with unforeseen consequences. Trying too hard to harness it risks eliminating it all together. Unfortunately for authoritarian regimes, the creative value-adding individuals, that at any rate appear few and far between, are often considered eccentric and quirky, not well adapted to authoritarianism. They are rebellious, even intimidating, and unafraid of confronting and questioning authority, both as embodied in their representatives and in the perceived truths around which society gyrates. To this point, some philosophical research papers have shown a linkage between creativity and transgressions, traits working in both directions. Thus, creativity may lead to deviousness, and deviousness can trigger creative solutions. Studies have shown that creative people are more likely to bend rules and even break laws.[19-21] Although this might be an odd observation and obviously disturbing from an ethical perspective, the term thinking out of the box can and should be loosely equated to thinking outside the existing rules.[22-24] Hence, creative thinking typically requires that one break some, but maybe not all, rules within a domain. This allows for and constructs associations between previously unconnected knowledge spheres. The resulting unusual mental conjunctions then serve as the basis for exploring and elaborating novel ideas. Research on creativity provides further evidence on what type of environment is conducive to prosperity from an innovative perspective. It includes removing organizational hindrances introduced through standardization of both process and people, and, in particular, being vigilant against an overabundance of rules and bureaucracy, because they lead to the summary rejection of many potentially good suggestions that could otherwise improve performance. Value-adding proposals, true to creative form, can often be nonlinear and unexpected, which, by default, rarely evokes appreciation, especially if they come from the wrong level (read: too junior) of the hierarchy.[25-28]

An authoritarian system, including a political one, is therefore highly inconducive to creative endeavors, because they are characterized by conformity. They are codified through hierarchical systems with a wide array of rules and regulations stipulating expected behavior. Any deviations thereof are often strongly condemned, and sometimes with fatal consequences. There are really no examples of authoritarian regimes under which creativity has been able to blossom over the longer term. It has proven very difficult to direct creativity into specific research areas while at the same time restricting it for others. Creativity, by its very nature, does not work that way, because creative individuals with rebellious personalities will sooner or later find themselves in trouble in a dictatorial society, and often, through deliberate provocations, come up with ideas that challenge what are considered unquestionable truths. The prerequisite for creativity, namely, a capacity for critical and probing thinking along with a disdain for absolute truths is rarely an appreciated faculty in a political system that rests on dogma that cannot be challenged without the risk of persecution. Through a repressive educational system, creative and rebellious natures are typically weeded out at an early stage, never being allowed to fully flourish and pursue their entrepreneurial and creative talents. For many self-censorship and repressing their own, and others, creative rebellious streaks become a survival tool. Of course, being fostered in an authoritarian setting, more often than not, these cultural tenets become so ingrained through parenting and the educational system that once they reach adulthood they are adhered to in an almost reflex-like manner, with little questioning of their usefulness. The rebellious and free-spirited *Steve Jobs* and *Elon Musk* characters of the world would struggle to fit into an authoritarian society and would likely never have been able to achieve what they have in the free-wielding American culture. At some point, they would have confronted the regime and various representatives of the bureaucracy with damaging consequences for them.

Concluding Thoughts

The effects of digitalization on society have been transpiring for a couple of decades already, but it is only in recent years that an increasingly clearer picture of what the future is shaping up to be has emerged. We are witnessing an economy with binary characteristics, and it is not an even split. A smaller segment of the workforce will thrive by being in demand for the foreseeable future to engage in digital transformations not only of the economy but also of society at large. However, there is a notable difference with respect to previous paradigm shifts. Being a digital worker is cognitively demanding, and there are constraints of an innate nature that exclude segments of the population from aspiring for roles in the digital economy. Without having a cognitive capacity for abstraction and analysis, and, ideally, the creative capability to innovate, one need not even apply. For the larger part of the population, the ambition cannot be higher than seeking to exist at the fringes of the digital economy because they cannot intellectually embrace the opportunities on offer. The future looks gloomy, to the point that for many there might not even be a future, in economic terms at least, to talk about. Participating in the labor market will be for them, at best, sporadic engagements, coinciding with the peaks and troughs of the economic cycles, or any governmental pushes to temporarily reduce unemployment numbers, typically occurring ahead of elections. It highlights a life with economic uncertainties that makes any long-term planning meaningless because it can only offer a meager hand-to-mouth existence. And there are quite literally signs of how fruitless this future is turning out to be for many. Contrary to conventional demographic wisdom but fulfilling a prophecy on nativity made a couple of centuries ago, birth rates for a destitute class of people on its way out have only one direction. But also, for the passengers on this proverbial gravy train are machines breathing down their necks. The digital workforce is increasingly being challenged by artificial intelligence tools, such as bots, which have seen their capacity to replicate human performances also in cognitively demanding areas advancing year by year. It has rendered more tasks susceptible to automation and becoming less reliant on human interventions. Thus, societies are adapting to new economic circumstances where the educational system, the coverage of the welfare system, and now also the demographics are undergoing dramatic change. The changes do not, however, stop there, because governing political models are likely to be impacted. The ethos that underpins much of digital transformation, which has taken inspiration from the agile philosophy, is to constantly and proactively challenge authority and ingrained ways of doing things. Disrupting processes through innovation has become a mantra to live by. The way forward has been staked out; attacking conventional truths and challenging authorities in whatever form have become means to progress. It is a mindset that will shape our culture for the foreseeable future and will eventually expand beyond merely taking aim at business models. Undoubtedly, it will also find its way into politics, hence authoritarian leaders, beware!

In all, the degree of changes we are now undergoing are perhaps unprecedented by historical standards. They are influencing so many aspects of our lives simultaneously that there is an urgent need for another style of leadership, in commerce and in politics. That leader is someone with the training and the mindset to view the world from a multitude of perspectives, which is essential to understand and stay on top of a highly complex and swiftly evolving environment. Most importantly, however, it is a leader that seeks to empower and enable humans rather than dictate. It appears that we have now reached the moment of *the renaissance of the renaissance man.*

Endnotes

1. H. Rindermann and J. Thompson. June 2011. "Cognitive Capitalism: The Effect of Cognitive Ability on Wealth, as Mediated through Scientific Achievement and Economic Freedom," *Psychological Science* 22, no. 6, pp. 754-63.

2. E.A. Hanushek. 2016. "Will More Higher Education Improve Economic Growth?" *Oxford Review of Economic Policy* 32, no. 4, pp. 538-552.

3. E.A. Hanushek and L. Wößmann. 2007. "Education Quality and Economic Growth," *The World Bank.* http://siteresources.worldbank.org /EDUCATION/Resources/278200-1099079877269/547664-1099079934475/Edu_Quality_Economic_Growth.pdf (accessed 1 June 2020)

4. H. Rindermann, M. Sailer, and J. Thompson. 2009. "The Impact of Smart Fractions, Cognitive Ability of Politicians and Average Competence of Peoples on Social Development." *Talent Development & Excellence* 1, no. 1, pp. 3-25. http://citeseerx.ist.psu.edu/viewdoc/ download?doi=10.1.1.397.4281&rep=rep1&type=pdf (accessed 1 June 2020).

5. H. Rindermann and J. Thompson. June 2011. "Cognitive Capitalism: The Effect of Cognitive Ability on Wealth, as Mediated through Scientific Achievement and Economic Freedom," *Psychological Science* 22, no. 6, pp. 754-63. https://www.ncbi.nlm.nih.gov/ pubmed/21537056 (accessed 1 June 2020).

6. H. Rindermann, M. Sailer, and J. Thompson. 2009. "The Impact of Smart Fractions, Cognitive Ability of Politicians and Average

Competence of Peoples on Social Development," *Talent Development & Excellence* 1, no. 1, pp. 3-25. http://citeseerx.ist.psu.edu/viewdoc/download?doi=10.1.1.397.4281&rep=rep1&type=pdf (accessed 1 June 2020).

7. R. Florida. 2002. "Bohemia and Economic Geography," *Journal of Economic Geography* 2, pp. 55-71. https://academic.oup.com/joeg/article-abstract/2/1/55/924231/Bohemia-and-economic-geography?redirectedFrom=fulltext (accessed 1 June 2020) .

8. I.J. Deary, A. Pattie, and J.M. Starr. December 2013. "The Stability of Intelligence from Age 11 to Age 90 Years: The Lothian Birth Cohort of 1921," *Psychological Science* 24, no. 12, pp. 2361-8.

9. I.J. Deary, M.C. Whiteman, A. Pattie, J.M. Starr, C. Hayward, A.F. Wright, A. Carothers, and L.J. Whalley. August 2002. "Ageing: Cognitive Change and the APOE e4 Allele," *Nature* 418, no. 6901, p. 932.

10. P. Beaudry, D.A. Green, and B.M. Sand. March 2013. "The Great Reversal in the Demand for Skill and Cognitive Tasks," NBER Working Paper No. 18901. http://www.nber.org/papers/w18901 (accessed 1 June 2020)

11. R.J. Mayhew. 2014. *Malthus: The Life and Legacies of an Untimely Prophet* (Cambridge, UK: Belknap Press), Chapter 2.

12. G. Meisenberg and M.A. Woodley of Menie. *Dysgenic Trends in the United States During the 20th Century: Toward Finding the Causes* [International Society for Intelligence Research (ISIR) 15th Annual Conference]. Graz, Austria, 2014.

13. F.E. Lindner and R.D. Grove. 1947. *Vital Statistics Rates in the United States 1900–1940* (Washington, DC: United States Government Printing Office).

14. S. Tavernise. 27 November 2019. "Fertility Rate in U.S. Hit a Record Low in 2018," *The New York Times*. https://www.nytimes.com/2019/11/27/us/us-birth-fertility-rate.html (accessed 1 June 2020)

15. G. Livingston. 22 May 2019. "Is U.S. Fertility at an All-time Low? Two of Three Measures Point to Yes," Pew Research Center. https://www.pewresearch.org/fact-tank/2019/05/22/u-s-fertility-rate-explained/ (accessed 1 June 2020).

16. L.B. Finer and M.R. Zolna. 2014. "Shifts in Intended and Unintended Pregnancies in the United States, 2001–2008," *American Journal of Public Health* 104, no. S1, pp. S43-S48.

17. S. Statistisk. 29 January 2014. "Fertility Rates and Other Demographics among Immigrants and Children of Immigrants Born in Norway." https://www.ssb.no/en/forskning/demografi-og-levekaar/fruktbarhet-ogfamiliedemografi/fertility-rates-and-other-demographicsamong-immigrants-and-children-of-immigrants-born-in-innorway (accessed 1 June 2020).

18. A. Pailhe. 27 April 2017. "The Convergence of Second-generation Immigrants' Fertility Patterns in France: The Role of Sociocultural Distance between Parents' and Host Country." *Demographic Research* 36, Article 45.

19. D.H. Cropley, J.C. Kaufman, and A.J. Cropley. 20 April 2008. "Malevolent Creativity: A Functional Model of Creativity in Terrorism and Crime," *Creativity Research Journal* 20, no. 2, pp. 105-15.

20. F.J. Sulloway. 1996. *Born to Rebel: Birth Order, Family Dynamics, and Creative Lives* (New York, NY: Pantheon Books).

21. F. Gino and S.S. Wiltermuth. 18 February 2014. "Evil Genius? How Dishonesty Can Lead to Greater Creativity," *Psychological Science* 25, no. 4.

22. J.P. Guilford. Winter 1967. "Creativity: Yesterday, Today and Tomorrow," *The Journal of Creative Behavior* 1, no. 1, pp. 3-14.

23. M.A. Runco. 2010. "Divergent Thinking, Creativity, and Ideation." In *The Cambridge Handbook of Creativity*, ed. J.C. Kaufman and R.J. Sternberg. New York, NY: Cambridge University Press, pp. 413-46.

24. D.K. Simonton. 1999. "Creativity as Blind Variation and Selective Retention: Is the Creative Process Darwinian?" *Psychological Inquiry* 10, no. 4, pp. 309-28.

25. S. Bailin. 1987. "Critical and Creative Thinking," *Informal Logic* 9, no. 1.

26. J.P. Guilford. 1950. "Creativity," *American Psychologist* 5, no. 9, pp. 444-54.

27. P. Langley and R. Jones. 1988. "A Computational Model of Scientific Insight." In *The Nature of Creativity: Contemporary Psychological Perspectives*, ed. R.J. Sternberg. Cambridge, UK: Cambridge University Press, pp. 177-201.

28. R.J. Sternberg. 1986. "A Triangular Theory of Love," *Psychological Review* 93, pp. 119-35.

Bibliography

Albert, R.S., and M.A. Runco. 1999. "A History of Research on Creativity." In *Handbook of Creativity*, ed. R.J. Sternberg. Cambridge: Cambridge University Press.

Ashmore, S., and K. Runyan. 2014. *Introduction to Agile Methods*. Boston, MA: Addison-Wesley.

Bailin, S. 1987. "Critical and Creative Thinking." *Informal Logic* 9, no. 1.

Beaudry, P., D.A. Green, and B.M. Sand. March 2013. "The Great Reversal in the Demand for Skill and Cognitive Tasks," NBER Working Paper No. 18901. http://www.nber.org/papers/w18901 (accessed 1 June 2020).

Beck, K., and C. Andres. 2004. *Extreme Programming Explained: Embrace Change (The XP Series)*. 2nd ed. Boston, MA: Addison-Wesley.

Beck, K., J. Grenning, R.C. Martin, M. Beedle, J. Highsmith, S. Mellor, A. van Bennekum, A. Hunt, K. Schwaber, A. Cockburn, R. Jeffries, J. Sutherland, W. Cunningham, J. Kern, D. Thomas, M. Fowler, and B. Marick. 2001. *Manifesto for Agile Software Development*. Corryton, TN: Agile Alliance.

Beck, K., J. Grenning, R.C. Martin, M. Beedle, J. Highsmith, S. Mellor, A. van Bennekum, A. Hunt, K. Schwaber, A. Cockburn, R. Jeffries, J. Sutherland, W. Cunningham, J. Kern, D. Thomas, M. Fowler, and B. Marick. 2001. *Principles behind the Agile Manifesto*. Corryton, TN: Agile Alliance.

Boden, M.A. 2004. *The Creative Mind: Myths and Mechanisms*. London, UK: Routledge.

Boehm, B., and R. Turner. 2004. *Balancing Agility and Discipline: A Guide for the Perplexed*. Boston, MA: Addison-Wesley.

Brosseau, D., S. Ebrahim, C. Handscomb, and S. Thaker. May 2019. "The Journey to an Agile Organization," McKinsey & Company. https://www.mckinsey.com/business-functions/organization/our-insights/the-journey-to-an-agile-organization (accessed 1 June 2020).

Burke, P. 2010. "The Polymath: A Cultural and Social History of an Intellectual Species." In *Explorations in Cultural History: Essays for Peter McCaffery*, ed. D.F. Smith and H. Philsooph. Aberdeen: Centre for Cultural History, University of Aberdeen.

Burke, P. 2012. *A Social History of Knowledge II: From the Encyclopaedia to Wikipedia*. Vol. 2, 1st ed. Cambridge, UK: Polity.

Castiglione, B. *The Book of the Courtier* (translated by Charles S. Singleton, New York: W.W. Norton, 2002) (original *Il Cortegiano*, Aldine Press, 1528).

Cropley, D.H., J.C. Kaufman, and A.J. Cropley. 20 April 2008. "Malevolent Creativity: A Functional Model of Creativity in Terrorism and Crime." *Creativity Research Journal* 20, no. 2, pp. 105-115.

Crowder J. and Freiss S. 2015. "The Psychology of Agile Team Leadership." Chapter in *Agile Project Management: Managing for Success*. Springer International Publishing.

Deary, I.J., A. Pattie, and J.M. Star. December 2013. "The Stability of Intelligence from Age 11 to Age 90 Years: The Lothian Birth Cohort of 1921." *Psychological Science* 24, no. 12, pp. 2361-8.

Deary, I.J., M.C. Whiteman, A. Pattie, J.M. Starr, C. Hayward, A.F. Wright, A. Carothers, and L.J. Whalley. August 2002. "Ageing: Cognitive Change and the APOE e4 Allele." *Nature* 418, no. 6901, p. 2.

Deemer, P., G. Benefield, C. Larman, and B. Vodde. 17 December 2012. "The Scrum Primer: A Lightweight Guide to the Theory and Practice of Scrum (Version 2.0)," *InfoQ*. https://www.infoq.com/minibooks/Scrum_Primer/ (accessed 1 June 2020).

Ebrahim, S., K. Krishnakanthan and S. Thaker. October 2018. "Harnessing Agile Compendium," McKinsey & Company. https://www.mckinsey.com/~/media/McKinsey/Business%20Functions/Organization/Our%20Insights/Harnessing%20agile%20compendium/Harnessing-Agile-compendium-October-2018.ashx (accessed 1 June 2020).

Ebstein, R.P., J. Benjamin, and R.H. Belmaker. 2003. "Behavioral Genetics, Genomics, and Personality." In *Behavioral Genetics in the Postgenomic Era*, ed. R. Plomin, J.C. DeFries, I.W. Craig, and P. McGuffin. Washington, DC: American Psychological Association.

Encyclopaedia Britannica. "Renaissance Man." https://www.britannica.com/topic/Renaissance-man (accessed 1 June 2020).

Finer, L.B., and M.R. Zolna. 2014. "Shifts in Intended and Unintended Pregnancies in the United States, 2001–2008." *American Journal of Public Health* 104, no. S1.

Florida, R. 2002. "Bohemia and Economic Geography." *Journal of Economic Geography* 2. https://academic.oup.com/joeg/article-abstract/2/1/55/924231/Bohemia-and-economic-geography?redirectedFrom=fulltext (accessed 1 June 2020).

Gabora, L. *Cognitive Mechanisms Underlying the Origin and Evolution of Culture* [Doctoral thesis]. Brussels, Belgium: Free University of Brussels; 2001).

Gardner, H. 1970. *Art through the Ages*. 5th ed. New York, NY: Harcourt, Brace & World.

Gilhooly, K.J. 2016. "Incubation and Intuition in Creative Problem Solving." *Frontiers in Psychology* 7, p. 1076.

Gino, F., and S.S. Wiltermuth. 18 February 2014. "Evil Genius? How Dishonesty Can Lead to Greater Creativity." *Psychological Science* 25, no. 4.

Gren, L. 2015. "Using the Work and Organizational Psychology Perspective in Research on Agile Software Development Teams," Computer Science. https://www.semanticscholar.org/paper/Using-the-Work-and-Organizational-Psychology-in-on-Gren/8634c226690fe73f0ee891f0e2d35a140a6f38e4 (accessed 1 June 2020).

Guilford, J.P. 1950. "Creativity." *American Psychologist* 5, no. 9.

Guilford, J.P. Winter 1967. "Creativity: Yesterday, Today and Tomorrow." *Journal of Creative Behavior* 1, no. 1.

Hanushek, E.A. 2016. "Will More Higher Education Improve Economic Growth?" *Oxford Review of Economic Policy* 32, no. 4.

Hanushek, E.A., and L. Wößmann. 2007. "Education Quality and Economic Growth," The World Bank. http://siteresources.worldbank.org/EDUCATION/Resources/278200-1099079877269/547664-1099079934475/Edu_Quality_Economic_Growth.pdf (accessed 1 June 2020)

Hollingsworth, R.J., and E.J. Hollingsworth. 2011. *Major Discoveries, Creativity, and the Dynamics of Science (Complexity Design Society, 15)*. Vienna, Austria: Remaprint Wien.

Iacocca Institute. 1991. *21st Century Manufacturing Enterprise Strategy: An Industry Led View*. Bethlehem, PA: Iacocca Institute, Lehigh University.

Kroll, C., L. Boeing, T. Schmidt, M. Vogg, T. Bastian, C. Lengfeld, and R. Rauch. August 2017. "Agile Organizations: An Approach for a Successful Journey towards More Agility in Daily Business," Capgemini Consulting. https://www.capgemini.com/consulting-de/wp-content/uploads/sites/32/2017/08/cc_agile_organization_pov_20170508.pdf (accessed 1 June 2020).

Kuhn, T.S. 1996. *The Structure of Scientific Revolutions*. 3rd ed. Chicago, IL: Chicago University Press.

Langley, P., and R. Jones. 1988. "A Computational Model of Scientific Insight." In *The Nature of Creativity: Contemporary Psychological Perspectives*, ed. R.J. Sternberg. Cambridge, UK: Cambridge University Press.

Lee, G., and W. Xia. 2010. "Toward Agile: An Integrated Analysis of Quantitative and Qualitative Field Data on Software Development Agility." *MIS Quarterly* 34, no. 1.

Lindner, F.E., and R.D. Grove. 1947. *Vital Statistics Rates in the United States 1900–1940*. Washington, DC: United States Government Printing Office.

Livingston, G. 22 May 2019. Is U.S. "Fertility at an All-time Low? Two of Three Measures Point to Yes," Pew Research Center. https://www.pewresearch.org/fact-tank/2019/05/22/u-s-fertility-rate-explained/ (accessed 1 June 2020).

Mayhew, R.J. 2014. *Malthus: The Life and Legacies of an Untimely Prophet.* Cambridge, MA: Belknap Press.

Meisenberg, G., and M.A. Woodley of Menie. *Dysgenic Trends in the United States during the 20th Century: Toward Finding the Causes* [International Society for Intelligence Research (ISIR) 15th Annual Conference]. Graz, Austria, 2014.

Moran, A. 2014. *Agile Risk Management.* Springer Verlag, Springer Briefs in Computer Science.

Moran, A. 2015. *Managing Agile: Strategy, Implementation, Organisation and People.* Berlin: Springer Verlag.

Musson, A.E., and E. Robinson. 1969. *Science and Technology in the Industrial Revolution.* Toronto, ON: University of Toronto Press.

Nelson, D. 1970. *Frederick W. Taylor and the Rise of Scientific Management.* Madison: MIT Press.

Nicolaou, N., and S. Shane. 2010. "Entrepreneurship and Occupational Choice: Genetic and Environmental Influences." *Journal of Economic Behavior & Organization* 76.

Nicolaou, N., and S. Shane. 2019. "Common Genetic Effects on Risk-taking Preferences and Choices." *Journal of Risk and Uncertainty* 59. https://link.springer.com/article/10.1007/s11166-019-09316-2 (accessed 1 June 2020).

Ochse, R. 1990. *Before the Gates of Excellence: The Determinants of Creative Genius.* New York, NY: Cambridge University Press.

Pailhe, A. 27 April 2017. "The Convergence of Second-Generation Immigrants' Fertility Patterns in France: The Role of Sociocultural Distance between Parents' and Host Country." *Demographic Research*, 36, Article 45.

Pichler, R. 2010. *Agile Product Management with Scrum: Creating Products that Customers Love.* Upper Saddle River, NJ: Addison-Wesley.

Poincaré, H. 1910. "Mathematical Creation." *The Monist* 20, no. 3, pp. 321-35.

Rao, L.L., Y. Zhou, D. Zheng, L.Q. Yang, and S. Li. 1 October 2018. "Genetic Contribution to Variation in Risk Taking: A Functional MRI Twin Study of the Balloon Analogue Risk Task." *Psychological Science* 29, no. 10. https://journals.sagepub.com/doi/10.1177/0956797618779961 (accessed 1 June 2020).

Rigby, D.K., J. Sutherland, and H. Takeuchi. May 2016. "Embracing Agile," Harvard Business Review. https://hbr.org/2016/05/embracing-agile (accessed 1 June 2020).

Rigby, D.K., S. Berez, G. Caimi, and A. Noble. 19 April 2016. "Agile Innovation," Bain & Company, Insights. https://www.bain.com/insights/agile-innovation/ (accessed 1 June 2020).

Rindermann, H., J. Thompson. June 2011. "Cognitive Capitalism: The Effect of Cognitive Ability on Wealth, as Mediated through Scientific Achievement and Economic Freedom." *Psychological Science* 22, no. 6. https://www.ncbi.nlm.nih.gov/pubmed/21537056 (accessed 1 June 2020).

Rindermann, H., M. Sailer, and J. Thompson. 2009. "The Impact of Smart Fractions, Cognitive Ability of Politicians and average Competence of Peoples on social Development." *Talent Development & Excellence* 1, no. 1. http://citeseerx.ist.psu.edu/viewdoc/download?doi=10.1.1.397.4281&rep=rep1&type=pdf (accessed 1 June 2020).

Root-Bernstein, R., and M.M. Root-Bernstein. 2011. "Life Stages of Creativity." In *Encyclopedia of Creativity, Reference Work*, ed. M.A. Runco and S.R. Pritzker. 2nd ed. Oxford: Elsevier.

Root-Bernstein, R., and M.M. Root-Bernstein. 2017. "People, Passions, Problems: The Role of Creative Exemplars in Teaching for Creativity." In *Creative Contradictions in Education, Cross Disciplinary Paradoxes and Perspectives*, ed. R.A. Beghetto and B. Sriraman. Berlin: SpringerLink.

Root-Bernstein, R. 2003. *The Art of Innovation: Polymaths and Universality of the Creative Process*. The international handbook on innovation.

Rothenberg, A., C.R. Hausman, and N. Durham. 1976. *The Creativity Question*. Durham: Duke University Press Books.

Rubin, K. 2013. *Essential Scrum. A Practical Guide to the Most Popular Agile Process*. Boston, MA: Addison-Wesley.

Runco, M.A. 2006. *Creativity and Reason in Cognitive Development*. Cambridge, UK: Cambridge University Press.

Runco, M.A. 2010. "Divergent Thinking, Creativity, and Ideation." In *The Cambridge Handbook of Creativity*, ed. J.C. Kaufman and R. J. Sternberg. New York, NY: Cambridge University Press.

Schwaber, K. 2004. *Agile Project Management with Scrum*. Microsoft Press, Developer Best Practices.

Shavinina, L. 2013. "How to Develop Innovators? Innovation Education for the Gifted." *Gifted Education International* 29, no. 1.

Simonton, D.K. 1999. "Creativity as Blind Variation and Selective Retention: Is the Creative Process Darwinian?" *Psychological Inquiry* 10, no. 4.

Sio, U.N., and T.C. Ormerod. January 2009. "Does Incubation Enhance Problem Solving? A Meta-analytic Review." *Psychological Bulletin* 135, no. 1.

Statistisk, S. 29 January 2014. "Fertility Rates and Other demographics among Immigrants and Children of Immigrants Born in Norway." https://www.ssb.no/en/forskning/demografi-og-levekaar/fruktbarhet-ogfamiliedemografi/fertility-rates-and-other-demographicsamong-immigrants-and-children-of-immigrants-born-innorway (accessed 1 June 2020).

Sternberg, R.J. 1986. "A Triangular Theory of Love." *Psychological Review* 93.

Sternberg, R., and T. Lubart. 1999. *The Concept of Creativity: Prospects and Paradigms. Handbook of Creativity*. London, UK: Cambridge University Press, Vol. 1.

Sulloway, F.J. 1996. *Born to Rebel: Birth Order, Family Dynamics, and Creative Lives*. New York, NY: Pantheon Books.

Tavernise, S. 27 November, 2019. "Fertility Rate in U.S. Hit a Record Low in 2018." *The New York Times*. https://www.nytimes.com/2019/11/27/us/us-birth-fertility-rate.html (accessed 1 June 2020).

Tetlock, P.E., and D. Gardner. 2015. *Superforecasting: The Art and Science of Prediction*. 1st ed. New York, NY: Crown.

Thorgren, S., and E. Caiman. 2019. "The Role of Psychological Safety in Implementing Agile Methods across Cultures." *Research-Technology Management* 62, no. 2. https://www.tandfonline.com/doi/full/10.1080/08956308.2019.1563436 (accessed 1 June 2020).

Törnqvist, G. 2004. *Kreativitetens geografi*. Stockholm: SNS Förlag.

Verheyen, G. 2013. *Scrum: A Pocket Guide (A Smart Travel Companion)*. Van Haren Publishing, Best Practice.

Wallas, G. 2014. *The Art of Thought*. Kent, UK: Solis Press.

About the Author

Niklas Hageback is a seasoned project manager/change leader with an expertise in agile methodologies. He has held regional executive management and project oversight roles at leading banks, including Credit Suisse, Deutsche Bank, and Goldman Sachs, in both Asia and Europe, where he was in charge of a number of complex regionwide digital transformation and risk management initiatives. More recently, he has done extensive work in artificial intelligence, notably machine learning, leading the development of automated human reasoning and computational creativity applications.

He is a published author with bestsellers including *The Virtual Mind: Designing the Logic to Approximate Human Thinking* (2017), and *The Death Drive—Why Societies Self-Destruct* (2020). He has also published a number of research papers in AI and finance.

Index

OTHER TITLES IN OUR COLLABORATIVE INTELLIGENCE COLLECTION

Jim Spohrer and Haluk Demirkan, *Editors*

- *Cultural Science: Applications of Artificial Social Intelligence* by William Sims Bainbridge
- *The Future of Work: How Artificial Intelligence Can Augment Human Capabilities* by Yassi Moghaddam, Heather Yurko, Haluk Demirkan, Nathan Tymann and Ammar Rayes
- *Advancing Talent Development: Steps Toward a T-Model Infused Undergraduate Education* by Philip Gardner and Heather N. Maietta
- *Virtual Local Manufacturing Communities: Online Simulations of Future Workshop Systems* by William Sims Bainbridge
- *T-Shaped Professionals: Adaptive Innovators* by Yassi Moghaddam, Haluk Demirkan and James Spohrer
- *The Interconnected Individual: Seizing Opportunity in the Era of AI, Platforms, Apps, and Global Exchanges* by Hunter Hastings and Jeff Saperstein

Concise and Applied Business Books

The Collection listed above is one of 30 business subject collections that Business Expert Press has grown to make BEP a premiere publisher of print and digital books. Our concise and applied books are for...

- Professionals and Practitioners
- Faculty who adopt our books for courses
- Librarians who know that BEP's Digital Libraries are a unique way to offer students ebooks to download, not restricted with any digital rights management
- Executive Training Course Leaders
- Business Seminar Organizers

Business Expert Press books are for anyone who needs to dig deeper on business ideas, goals, and solutions to everyday problems. Whether one print book, one ebook, or buying a digital library of 110 ebooks, we remain the affordable and smart way to be business smart. For more information, please visit **www.businessexpertpress.com**, or contact **sales@businessexpertpress.com**.

www.ingramcontent.com/pod-product-compliance
Lightning Source LLC
Chambersburg PA
CBHW052109230326
41599CB00054B/5273